The Listen Lady

Annie has baked a sumptuous cupcake of a story using all the mysterious ingredients of social media to illustrate practical marketing applications that any entrepreneur could understand and apply to make their business more successful.

Cam Davis, Ph.D. @CamDavis48, Managing Director of Social Data Research

The book is a lovely, easy read which neatly identifies, lists and extols the key pillars of our Social Media ethics and tops them off with a nice little analytical "cherry."

Finn Raben, @Finn01, Director General of ESOMAR

FANTASTIC! Very clever wording choices, phrases. Imagery is excellent. Crystal is someone I relate to.

Kathryn Korostoff, @ResearchRocks, President of Research Rockstar, Author of How to Hire & Manage Market Research Agencies

Annie manages to place a real-world stepwise guide to conducting social media research in a clever fictionalized novel form. This book is great for business and research managers alike. Well worth the read!

Vaughn Mordecai, @Discores, President of Discovery Research Group, Author of The Landmark Blog

A sure sign of the times" – proof that social media research has come of age, a "how to" book has been written in a light hearted way by no less than our favourite blogger, LoveStats. A "must read" for aspiring social media analysts.

Tessie Ting, @TessieTweets, Co-Founder of Conversition

The LoveStats Blog Volume 1: 2009

Coming in 2012
The LoveStats Blog Volume 2: 2010
The LoveStats Blog Volume 3: 2011

The Listen Lady

A novel and
social media research guide
baked into one

F. Annie Pettit PhD

Dedicated To

Dustin who gives me heart

The Conversition team, Tessie Ting, and Jean Davis who give me wings

The Twitteratti who give me reason

The MRIA, MRA, CASRO, and ESOMAR who give me faith

The
Listen Lady

To Denise
My newest, bestest friend
and fellow towny

Love Annie

Chapter 1.

After an hour of painstakingly tweaking decimal places and fiddling with equations on her laptop, Crystal sat behind her desk at the window attempting a popular technique called 'staring at the numbers until your eyes explode.' Perpetually tired from fifteen hour work days, Crystal found easy success in the task. She rested her chin in her hands and allowed her blank gaze to shift to the city outside.

Past her bakery and the neighbouring shops, college kids weighted down with MEC knapsacks hurried through the downtown street on their way to class. Fitness freaks in Lulu Lemons speed-walked to the local fitness club three streets over. A row of newly planted red Maple trees, an attempt by local residents to bring life to the neighbourhood, lined the sidewalk but with leaves yet to fill out, could not bring life to the tired street.

Their heads down, braced against the crisp breeze, passers-by paid no attention to the tiny bakery stuffed between a mani-pedi shop, its windows covered in faded brown paper and a second-hand bookstore that strangely proclaimed Cheep Cheep Prices. Above the bakery door, a newly hand-painted sign of a sweet, gray-haired Grannie greeted all who chanced to look up. And today, one person did.

The front door of Grannie's swung open smacking the door chime into action and Crystal out of her stupor. She slammed her laptop closed and sprang lightly to her feet. Not a miniscule crumb fell from her whiter than white apron as she brushed her hands across it and smoothed it flat over her precision pressed white shirt and khakis. Her blonde hair, tightly packed into a pony-tail with not a single stray strand, was the vanilla icing on a non-fat, non-sugar, flavourless cupcake.

"Morning," she called out, relieved that the aroma of this morning's triple fudge brownies had lingered long enough to greet her visitor. "Welcome to Grannie's." Crystal pulled a fresh pair of thin plastic gloves from her apron pocket and yanked them on. She stood at attention behind the counter, a dutiful smile on her face.

"Good morning," replied the customer as the door creaked shut behind her. She pushed aside the sleeve of her woollen jacket and checked her watch. "Lunch time, it is." She took in the narrow shop in one prolonged gaze.

A long, red brick wall covered with an expanse of adjustable IKEA shelves held a few fat loaves of pumpernickel bread, some sourdough rounds cut with cross hatches, and six paper bags of whole wheat sandwich bread. The opposite wall boasted drywall the colour of every hotel room that ever existed and served as the backdrop for a long glass dessert case. Inside the case, a limited assortment of heart attack inducing treats was on display. Almond nougat rounds with chocolate drizzle, gooey raisin buttertarts with flaky crusts, and cinnamon cookies shedding giant crystals of sugar tempted the eyes and the stomach.

Crystal's practiced smile remained firm as she sized up her new customer and decided on a suitable nickname. The short mousy hair, muted orange jacket, mustard yellow shoes, maroon cords, and forest green scarf combined to create an outfit that was either direct from the runway in Paris or a falsely benevolent cousin's cast-offs.

The crayon coloured lady turned to Crystal, letting the broad handle of her canvas bookbag slide off her shoulder and into her hand. "You must have had a busy morning." She nodded towards the sparse shelves. "You're almost sold out of everything but what I do see looks delicious."

"Thanks," Crystal said, her voice flat. "What can I get for you?" She picked up a flattened sheet of white cardboard from under the dessert case and folded it into a ten by ten pie box.

Leaning forward to peer into the dessert cases, the Crayon Lady pointed at a tray of meticulously arranged date squares finished with a crumbly oatmeal topping. "Two of those. I've never been able to resist a chunky date square and those look like the best I've ever seen."

With a slight sigh, Crystal replaced the pie box under the counter and instead folded together a smaller box. She tucked both squares into the box and tied it securely with a long pink string.

As she waited, the Crayon Lady picked up one of the business cards displayed the cash register. She glanced at the Grannie's logo on the front of the card, and quickly flipped the card over and back again. "What's your Twitter name?" she asked, looking up at Crystal. "It's not on your card."

Crystal stared for a moment at the Crayon Lady and then at the stack of business cards. She was puzzled by the question having double and triple checked every letter and number before finally approving their printing. She knew there was nothing wrong with them.

"My what?" Crystal finally asked, doubt building in her mind. She picked up a card for herself, checking it letter by letter again.

"Your Twitter name. You're on Twitter, no?"

Crystal turned her head from side to side, slowly, her face full of confusion.

The Crayon Lady crammed the card into her jacket pocket, the sound of crinkling echoing through the bakery. "Let me guess. You don't know what Twitter is. I'm on Twitter so much that I forget barely thirteen percent of people who use the internet use Twitter. And you're one of the people who should."

Glancing around the bakery once more before turning back to Crystal, she continued. "It smells fantastic in here, like you've baked a teaspoon of Grannie's love into everything. You really should get online and take advantage of social media. Twitter would be the perfect way to promote your bakery to thousands of people." With the small white box tucked safely inside her worn bag, she winked at Crystal and departed.

Sure, Crystal thought, as she watched the Crayon Lady disappear down the street. That's the quick fix I need. Playing on the internet will fix everything.

Chapter 2.

As the door creaked shut and the street sounds quieted to nothing behind the closed door, Crystal pulled the rickety garage-sale stool out from under her desk and slumped into it.

As a kid, she had filled her spare time baking crumble-topped cranberry muffins and perfectly smooth cherry cheesecakes, treats that were sought after and devoured by friends and colleagues who had a bit of spare cash to cover the cost of ingredients. Every crack and every cranny in her mother's kitchen had been perpetually embedded with flour and sugar no matter how diligently Crystal cleaned up after her creative endeavours.

Her passion for baking turned into a dream and eventually a dream fund into which every penny earned from babysitting and odd painting jobs was squirreled away. When she was old enough to command minimum wage and tips, the dream fund grew more quickly from waitressing and working in the bakery of a local grocery store. Building the dream fund superseded the manicures, celebrity gossip magazines, and venti double-shot lattes that her highschool classmates splurged on. Instead, Crystal treated herself with professional quality baking equipment and parchment paper.

With an overdose of determination, a Baking and Pastry Arts Diploma fresh in hand, and just enough money to cover rent and essentials, Crystal found herself the proud proprietor of 365 square feet of scratched paint, dirty floors, and musty air.

Leading up to opening day, Crystal polished and preened every square millimetre of what was sure to be the most beloved shop in the neighbourhood. She dreamed of impatient customers craning their heads to see in the windows at 6am, and shelves that were never full no matter how much she baked. She envisioned a staff of three part-timers bustling behind the counter, struggling to keep up with the steady stream of customers. Though opening day was a dream come true, each passing day and week chipped and tore at the dream. The shelves were practically empty not because there were so many customers but because there were no customers.

The unsolicited compliments from the Crayon Lady simply brought disappointment to the forefront of Crystal's mind and now, she sat at her desk harbouring her sorrows. She needed a distraction and a tiny red blinking light did the trick. Crystal tilted her head towards the laptop. It blinked again.

Blink. Blink.

It called to her, not to revise her financial predictions for the fiftieth time nor to revise her recipe for lactose-free brownies. It called to her to find out what the tweeter thing was, to discover what the Crayon Lady was talking about.

Crystal shimmied her stool closer to the desk and dragged the laptop a little closer. She opened up Firefox and typed a word into the Google search box. Staring at the first of 12 billion results, she could think of no better option than to click on the first one. This must be it, she thought.

Hopeful that the website would lead her down the right path, Crystal did as it instructed. She entered her name and email address, and chose a username. She proceeded through the pages and clicked on the follow button beside the oddly familiar names of Lady Gaga, Ryan Seacrest, Russell Brand, Charlie Sheen, and Katy Perry and more.

It didn't matter that the tweeter idea had come from a stranger. Crystal was not about to ignore any suggestion that could turn out to be the one thing between her and success. After completing the sign-up process, she twirled her index finger in the air and then clicked on the button that would bring everything to light.

HotGirl

OMG! Hot guy alert! Underwear is totally coming off right now!

TheOnlyOne

Movie comes out Friday. Check it. Worth every penny

MadeMillions

I made millions by following these five easy steps. You can too. Click here! http://bit.ly/46GHJdf

Kickinit

So pcker cn ply nd reply on twitter quick as bitch bt cnt **txt me**

Crystal's hand flew to her wide-open mouth. She burst out laughing at words that would normally result in a mouth full of soap. Resisting the urge to slam the laptop shut, she continued to read, sorting the messages into those written by crazy people, really crazy people, and those who had never had any marbles.

Intrigued at the types of messages that others had deemed worthy of sharing, Crystal delved deeper into the psyche of famous musicians, movie stars, and celebrity wanna-bes. A relationship break-up over a blue guitar. A new reality TV show about building fashionable furniture out of garbage. Falling down drunk in the middle of the road with no pants on. The messages were oddly addictive but for all the writing people did, there seemed to be little of substance.

Having learned as much as could possibly be learned, Crystal glanced at the time on her computer. She gasped in horror and slammed the laptop shut. Sure, she sometimes had trouble filling her days with useful activities but this was a new low. She hadn't found any new cost savings. She hadn't written any new recipes. She'd applied for no small business grants. She had, however, accomplished one thing. She'd gotten sucked into a nonsense website full of ridiculous gossip and wasted hours of valuable time. Just because a strange lady off the street told her to.

Crystal slid off the stool and, reaching under the counter, pulled out an empty packing box. She filled it with the day's unsold baked goods and carefully printed across the top with a thick black marker. At least the Daily Bread Food Bank would have a good day.

Chapter 3

The week progressed with early morning baking, mid-morning cleaning, and the dreaded afternoon task of packing up unsold date squares, apple tarts, and oatmeal cookies. This morning, the bread and treats baked, iced, and meticulously organized in the dessert case and on the shelves, Crystal wondered how much of it would end up in a packing box. She adjusted her hairnet confirming that every last strand of hair was securely jailed, washed her hands, and swapped her spotless apron for an immaculate one. She settled into her stool at the front window ready to concoct tasks for the rest of the day.

It was nearing one o'clock when the door chime pulled her away from an internet search for red Valentine's Day cookies that used no food colouring. Desperate to make the first sale of the day, she slammed the laptop closed and called out a cheerful "Morning." Crystal smoothed her apron and pulled on a fresh pair of plastic gloves before looking up to see she had a repeat customer.

"Hi again." The Crayon Lady strode over to the counter and deposited herself in front of the cash register. Like the week before, she gazed around the shop, taking in the pristine floors, the shiny glass cases, and the crumb-free counters. "My, my, it's quiet," she said, an easy smile on her face. "Is it always this quiet on Tuesdays?"

Crystal forced a smile. A huge lump filled her throat. "Uh, yeah. It's a bit quiet. Kind of cold out. No fun for shopping." Crystal waved her hand towards the window as three maroon-haired ladies strolled by clutching shopping bags.

"By the way," said the Crayon Lady, "I'm Brooke. Brooke Audire." She thrust a hand over the counter and grabbed Crystal's still rising hand. Shocked, Crystal managed to spit out her name.

"Did you take my advice?" Brooke asked. "I looked for you on Twitter and Facebook and Wordpress this week but I couldn't find you anywhere." Brooke paused for a moment. "Maybe I spelled Grannie's Goodies wrong."

"Well, I did sign up for it." Crystal chose her words carefully, working hard to ensure her voice was calm and polite. "I signed up for the tweeter and I even tried it out for a bit. Actually, I wasted a few hours on it." Crystal fiddled with the overly-long fingers of her plastic gloves.

Brooke leaned against the counter and tilted her head towards the glass case. "I don't remember seeing those the last time I was here." She nodded at a plate of buttertarts prominently displayed on top of the case.

"They were there," Crystal said. "I make a new kind of buttertarts every Tuesday." She watched Brooke peer into the case and tried to anticipate what she might buy this time. Date squares again, maybe the buttertarts? Anything?

"So you have a brand new kind of buttertart every Tuesday," repeated Brooke, still eyeing the contents of the dessert case.

Crystal nodded.

"A new kind of buttertart every Tuesday."

Crystal's eyes widened and she nodded again, more slowly this time. Apparently Brooke had squeaked through Kindergarten with a D in Listening.

"Who knows about your buttertart Tuesdays? How many people come in every Tuesday specifically to buy them?"

A moment of indecision preceded Crystal's answer. "One." The heat of embarrassment crept up her neck and spread across her cheeks. Something wasn't right. This Brooke person had something on her mind. She seemed to be looking for a specific answer.

"Would you like a way to tell hundreds of people, maybe even thousands of people, that Tuesdays are the best days to come by if you love buttertarts? Even better," she said, glancing around the immaculately maintained bakery, "since I've yet to see any customers in here, would you be interested in something free?"

Crystal wiped an invisible speck of dust from the top of the cash register. "Things will pick up soon. Grannie's is new. People haven't found it yet."

With a quiet look of understanding on her face, Brooke stood firm. She watched Crystal. She waited.

If Crystal had started the day with any confidence, it had melted away in the presence of this stranger. She knew it no longer mattered what secrets were spilled now. Brown paper in the windows would reveal them soon enough.

Crystal's cracked facade broke. "If you have to know, my bakery isn't doing well at all. I put every penny I ever earned to get this place and I'm going to lose everything."

Brooke's hands lay still against the edge of glass case, the frayed straps of her bookbag digging into her shoulder, threatening to spill the contents across the floor.

"I can't keep it up much longer," Crystal continued, surprised to feel the lump in her throat lessen. Sharing her secret felt good. The burden seemed more manageable.

Looking straight into Crystal's eyes, Brooke's voice was measured and authoritative. "I want to help you. I know it makes no sense to you but I can help you save your bakery. And it won't cost you anything."

Crystal fidgeted with her gloves. Strangers hold doors, pick up dropped items, and smile as you walk past them. Strangers don't come out of nowhere and offer to help you save your business. She glanced out the window wondering if she was on TV but saw no cameras, no lights, nothing unusual.

"Here's what I propose," Brooke continued. "Over the next couple of months, I'm going to visit your shop every

Tuesday around lunchtime and teach you what I know about using social media and market research to build a better business. I'll teach you how to learn about your industry, and how to research what your customers really want from you. My goal is that you end up with more customers, more money in your cash register, and hopefully so much business that you'll need to hire some help." Brooke took a small step back and folded her arms.

Crystal raised an eyebrow but said nothing. Keep talking, she thought.

Brooke outlined the rest of her plan. "My help isn't free."

Here it is, Crystal thought. Lay it on me.

"Every time we meet, instead of paying me for my time and advice, you'll pay me with a box of baking. You get free advice. I get free baking." Brooke stepped closer without losing eye contact. "You have nothing to lose," she encouraged.

Crystal couldn't believe it. This woman had obviously forgotten her wallet. All this for free cookies? She needed her bakery to succeed but she wasn't sure if she'd been offered something for nothing or nothing for something. Thoughts of fear and hope and bewilderment swirled around her head.

"Do we have a deal?" Brooke asked, her voice more authoritative and insistent now.

The faint hope that a mysterious plan might turn her failed shop into a success was as enticing to Crystal as vanilla flavouring made with Chopin vodka and eight plump Mexican vanilla beans. It had never been part of the plan to watch her lifelong dream disappear in three months. She couldn't let that happen if there was the slightest chance of preventing it. For the price of a box of baking.

"I'm in," Crystal said. The sound of her own voice accepting help surprised her. She felt a smile grow on her face.

"I'm glad to hear it. We start right now. Bring that." Brooke pointed at the laptop, spun on her heel, and marched to the back of the store where three mismatched chairs argued with a tiny table for space against the back wall. She squeezed herself into the wobbly blue chair and dumped her bag on the pristine floor.

Crystal stared after her self-invited guest. She watched, eyes wide open, as Brooke removed her scarf, jammed it in her bookbag, and settled in.

"Let's go," demanded Brooke, beckoning furiously to Crystal with her hand. "You aren't bogged down with customers and I don't have to be anywhere for an entire hour. Let's go."

After locking the cash register, Crystal pulled the key out and shoved it deep into her apron pocket. She covered it with two plastic gloves and an order pad, and nervously made her way to the table with the laptop.

Crystal had barely arrived at the table when Brooke reached out and grabbed the laptop with both hands. Crystal's grasp on her $200 refurbished purchase tightened.

Releasing her grip, Brooke laughed and held her hands up in mock defeat. "Relax. If I was that desperate for a netbook, I would have grabbed it last week."

Crystal smiled a narrow smile of nervousness and tentatively offered the laptop to Brooke. She pulled out a chair and sat down. "Why are you helping me?" she asked. "You can't be doing this just for free cookies. What's in this for you?"

"How about you worry about me after we turn your bakery into a massive success," Brooke said. "Are you one hundred percent on board?"

Crystal nodded sharply, an attempt to convince herself in the process. "Yeah. Let's go." She smoothed out her apron, discretely checking that the key remained firmly tucked inside the pocket.

Lesson one," Brooke said. "Let's start at the very beginning. First, you need to understand market research data. You need to know what it looks like, where it comes from, why it gets created. I'm going to train you to become a social media researcher and the first step is immersing yourself in social media data." She punctuated every word with hand gestures and pointing.

The lofty elocution lulled Crystal into dreamland. She wondered if she had the ingredients to make spiced brownies. She was pretty sure she had a full box of cranberries in the cupboard.

Oblivious, Brooke proceeded with her spur of the moment lesson. "Today, I'm going to introduce you to an easy website that will let you listen to and talk with the people who matter the most to you, potential customers. We're going to start with Twitter."

The dreaded word yanked Crystal out of her trance. She rolled her eyes in recollection of the educational virtues of the site. "Been there. Done that. No need." She slouched back in her chair, nearly banging into the dessert counter mere inches behind her. "Not interested in the tweeter." She mentally removed one brownie from Brooke's payment box.

"It sounds to me like you've experienced the stereotypical side of Twitter as opposed to the useful side of Twitter." Brooke opened Firefox and manoeuvred to the website. The login page greeted her with Crystal's username but not her password.

"If you click this button here," Brooke said, pointing to a tiny box near the login section, "Twitter will save a little file on your computer and you won't have to type your password in every time."

"Cool. Passwords are so annoying." Crystal mentally deposited half of a Brownie back into the payment box, the precisely calculated value of that tidbit of knowledge, and typed in her password.

"Let's see what you've got in your Twitter stream." Brooke flipped through the messages on Crystal's home page. "It looks like you're following a bunch of... shall we say, interesting people." She grinned and turned to Crystal.

"The computer told me to follow those people - "

"- and if everyone jumped off a bridge," Brooke teased, mimicking every mother who had ever reprimanded a twelve year old child. "This website has no idea what your business goals and objectives are. I'm sure your objective is not to learn about celebrity gossip but rather to learn about your consumers, and this," she pointed to the first message on the screen, "will not do it."

SteveMeyes

C3PO is the best droid bar none

"Hey, I agree with him," Crystal said, enjoying the Star Wars nostalgia.

"I'm glad to hear it," Brooke said. "But I'm not here to waste your time and you can't afford to waste your time." She pushed the laptop a few inches across the table to Crystal. "Unfollow all of those people."

With only slight reluctance, Crystal unfollowed the celebrities. Except for one. "Actually," she said, pausing at one account, "I want to keep this one. This popcornface guy is kinda funny. He shows pieces of popcorn that look like people." She peeked out at Brooke from the corner of her eye and eased the cursor away from the Unfollow button.

"That, my dear, is Twitter rule number one," Brooke said. "A major part of social media is engaging with people who resonate with you. If someone makes you laugh, follow them. If someone warms your heart, follow them. If someone helps you learn about your industry, follow them. So keep popcornface on your list. Social media can be useful *and* fun."

"That sounds nice and all," Crystal said, "but I've already seen how useful Twitter is. You've got a long way to go to convince me of that."

"Understood," Brooke continued. "My task then is to find the right people for you to listen to, people who love what you love, people who love baking and bread and dessert."

Under Brooke's guidance, Crystal clicked through the Twitter screens and followed a new collection of people. But not musicians, movie stars, sports celebrities. This time, she built a collection of average, everyday people who owned and managed and worked in bakeries, pastry shops, bread shops, cupcake shops, and chocolate shops, a group of people who shared her love and passion for running a bakery.

Then, they found Twitter accounts representing the Baking Association of Canada, the National Confectioners Association, and the Cupcake Bakers Association. From now on, Crystal would hear the industry news the moment it was released from the people who actually released it.

Finally, Crystal followed one more important group of people. After typing Toronto into the search box, Crystal read through the messages and followed people who tweeted about Toronto and food together. These VIPs would be her potential customers, the people who might decide to visit her bakery.

In less than an hour, Brooke and Crystal had built a Twitter account that followed more than three hundred people.

"Now what?" Crystal asked, turning to Brooke. "Now we find out what movies these people watched last night? What kind of Poptarts they had for breakfast? If they went to the bathroom?"

Brooke chuckled. "There you go with your preconceived notions. This is why you need to outline your objectives when you begin using social media. If you build your network to meet your objectives, interesting things will happen. Look at your Twitter stream now."

On her home page, Crystal found a long list of messages waiting to be read. She skimmed over the first few messages but this time, something was different. The messages weren't about cereal and swearing. The polite smile on her face disappeared. By the time she'd read another ten messages, a new smile appeared on her face, one of genuine excitement.

PrincessBakery

Smells so good! Pumpernickel bread just came out of the oven. You can't resist!

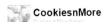

CookiesnMore

Found a great new recipe site. Take a peek! http://bit.ly/id9e3uh

SweetTreats

This picture of Nanaimo bars is going to make you drool. http://www.tr.wl/d8euek

Challah

The next five customers get a free Challah!

Wheatons

Bread is our thing but we dare you to try our cakes!

SugarAndSpice

We're opening a second location! Stay tuned for more info.

Crystal leaned into the laptop, her eyes jumping from message to message. She saw links to new recipes, pictures of artisan bread, menu suggestions, and chatter about chocolate chip cookies fresh out of the oven. Customers applauded their favourite bakeries and bakers applauded their favourite baked goods. Crystal felt like she was reading a fifty page newspaper with articles hand-picked for her.

"Wow." Crystal finally pulled herself away from the screen. Excited anticipation burst from every pore on her face. "I thought Twitter was a bunch of crazy people talking about stupid stuff. I had no idea it was like this."

Brooke tilted her head and smiled. "Look at this." She pointed to the top of Crystal's page. "You joined Twitter a few days ago and already you've got a follower count of one. Someone is waiting to listen to everything you have to say."

"What? Someone's following me?" As far as she knew, Crystal didn't know anyone on Twitter. It was kind of creepy to know that someone was waiting to listen to her.

"That's the whole point of social media," Brooke said. "You follow a few hundred people and a few hundred people follow you. But, I'm not sure why this person is following you." Brooke clicked through to a different section of Crystal's page. "Because this is your Twitter profile."

Crystal Olivia
@Crystal4758

Crystal shook her head. "Yuck." She didn't know much about this tweeter thing but she knew this wasn't good.

"Agreed. It's the default profile that gets assigned to every new account. It's acceptable in the beginning when you're still figuring things out, but it will not work for you. We're going to fix it so that more people will discover that you're a great person to chat with."

Brooke fished into her jacket pocket and, from among various scraps of paper, selected a small, wrinkled card which she showed to Crystal. "Have you got a digital copy of this little lady?"

"Yeah." Crystal was surprised to see her well-worn business card. She quickly found the image on her laptop and watched as Brooke uploaded it to Twitter as Crystal's new avatar.

"Most people use a picture of their face as their avatar," Brooke explained. "It helps people connect with you and feel like they're talking to a real person, not a brick wall."

"So why didn't you use my picture then?" Crystal squinched her face at Brooke. "Aren't I pretty enough for the internet?"

"That's exactly it," Brooke joked. "In your case, it has everything to do with branding. First of all, we want to use social media to generate brand recognition and familiarize people with the Grannie's brand. When they see that logo on your front door, they'll already recognize you from your social media presence. Second, you're not going to hide behind your logo. A lot of people engage in social media on behalf of their company, and the account ends up shovelling out dry information that never lets you feel a connection with the person behind the curtain. There's no personality, no creativity. You, on the other hand, are going to let your Grannie personality come through loud and clear. Right?"

Crystal nodded and fidgeted in her seat. She straightened her apron on her lap making sure the left and right sides hung in equal proportion. "Yup, I'll let my personality come through." Whatever that meant.

"That's not convincing at all," Brooke said with a stern face. "You need to write your messages in the same way you talk. Don't force a professional voice with formal grammar if that's not how you really talk. If you think something is way cool, don't say it's particularly interesting and noteworthy, and if you think your tarts are sticky and gooey, don't say that people should be cautious or they will stain their attire."

"Like C3PO and popcornface." Crystal finally clued in to the distinction.

"Exactly," Brooke said. "You need to be yourself and have a little fun. That's who you are and that's why people will want to listen to you and chat with you. Make it easy for people to get to know you and your shop, and you'll learn a lot of valuable information in return."

"Got it." Crystal was game to give it one more try but she wondered how long it would take to get bored with the tweeter this time. If it failed again, she'd have no choice but to resort to plan b, c, and d, whatever those would turn out to be.

"Alright, your logo looks great here. Now we need to write a quick description about Grannies Goodies in 160 characters or less. KISS me."

"What?" Crystal turned towards the woman she barely knew, worried that a pucker of bright red lips would suddenly appear.

"You look awfully nervous." The look on Brooke's face suggested her intention was otherwise. "I'm disappointed. Just keep the description of Grannies short and simple. KISS."

"Shoot, you had me there," Crystal said, grinning.

Like a game of Scrabble played to the death, Crystal and Brooke swapped important key words back and forth until they had created the perfect description of Grannies.

"We have one more important item to change and then we're done," Brooke said. "You need a username that instantly cues people to Grannies, a name that is easy to remember, easy to find, and slightly more descriptive than Crystal4758." After a quick search to confirm their preference was available, Brooke made the final edit to Crystal's account.

"Here, my dear, is your official profile." Brooke presented the final result to Crystal. "Remember the old one? What do you think now?"

Crystal Olivia
@GranniesGoodies Toronto

Cookies, brownies, squares, tarts, and bread. Home baked every morning with love by Grannie. 112 Yonge Street, Toronto

"I love it." Crystal silently clapped her hands. "That's way better than before."

"I'm glad to hear it." Brooke stared Crystal straight in the eye.

"What?" Crystal was nervous about Brooke's sneaky look.

"Are you ready?" Brooke asked.

"Ready for what?" Crystal pulled back from the table. This couldn't be good.

"For a momentous occasion. This will be the first time people hear your voice, the first time you tweet, a tweet that will live on forever. Are you ready to tweet your first real tweet?"

Crystal froze in terror.

Chapter 4

Crystal's premonition had been justified. Logically, she knew that at some point she would have to tweet. She just didn't think it would be so soon or so sudden. "I don't have anything to say," she finally relented.

"That's a terrible excuse," Brooke said. "You have an abundance of things to say. There's a pile of recipe cards on your desk and you baked some gorgeous bread. You could easily share a new recipe or photograph every day and have people drooling out of your hands. You have plenty to share."

Crystal blushed at the compliment. She had hundreds of pictures on her computer, a digital scrapbook of every recipe she'd ever tried. If she shared one picture every day, she'd have more than enough things to say for an entire year.

"Besides," Brooke said, "you're reading everyone else's tweets so it's only fair that you contribute something in return. What do you want the world to know about Grannie's Goodies?"

"The world?" Crystal's face paled and the lump in her throat returned bigger than ever.

"Yes, the world. Anything you type here can be read by anyone on the internet, anywhere in the world, from this day forward to the end of time, Amen. Social media isn't just your friends or your town. It's the world."

"You're making me nervous." Crystal squirmed in the uncomfortable wooden chair.

"Don't worry about it," Brooke said. "The rules are simple. Don't share anything that you don't feel comfortable sharing. Stick to bakery equipment, recipes, and pictures of your baking and you can't go wrong. Be yourself and be nice. And don't swear."

"Oh come on, I don't swear." Crystal feigned shock at the suggestion.

"I noticed that," Brooke said, "but you need to realize that the internet is a massive repository for profanity, racism, sexism, homophobia, and every mean, nasty, rude, and crude thing you can and can't imagine. If that kind of language bothers you, then social media research isn't for you."

"I'm fine with it," Crystal giggled. "I've seen what people say on the internet and it's not that bad." Brooke clearly liked to exaggerate.

"I'm sure you're fine with the standard profanity," Brooke said. "People might use the F word or S word, or even pretty them up by saying fawk or fugg, or shate or shyte, but it can get far worse. Don't be caught off guard when you do see it."

"That's silly," Crystal said. "Swearing is still swearing even if you spell it differently. I can think of a million other ways to spell those words."

"No need to procrastinate. What was the last thing that came out of the oven this morning? Did you try a new recipe today? If you had a hundred customers in your store right now, what would you tell them?"

Crystal scanned the bakery, waiting for the perfect idea to present itself. "I should tweet about the buttertarts, right?" She cocked her head and accepted a the nod of encouragement. She put her fingers on the F and J keys and typed.

"Come buy buttertarts at Grannies Goodies!"

With a nervous grin, Crystal ceremoniously held her index finger over the enter key and looked over to see Brooke shaking her head.

"Is that the tone you want for your bakery?" Brooke asked.

The virtual slap on the hand stung and Crystal yanked her hands away from the keyboard. "No, definitely not." She didn't know why it wasn't a good message but she could tell she was about to find out.

"Good answer. You don't want to use social media for overt sales pitches. You want to intrigue people, encourage friendships, show people why they want to listen to you. Erase that terrible tweet and try again."

Crystal backspaced over the unsent message. She knew the buttertarts were the right focus and she imagined taking a bite, flakey bits of golden pastry fluttering to the floor, and warm, gooey filling oozing over her fingers. Crystal wiggled her fingers in anticipation and typed out a message. She hit the Enter key without waiting for approval.

GranniesGoodies

A new gooey butter tart every Tuesday. Are your fingers sticky yet?

"I did it," Crystal exclaimed.

"And it's a great sharable tweet, short, and sweet in every sense of the word," Brooke said. "As long as you write genuine messages like this, people will feel like they're right here in Grannies with you. You know, in the olden days, before email and internet and instant messaging, you'd have to spend thousands of dollars to rent billboard space, print flyers, or make a TV commercial to share that message beyond your immediate friends. You wrote something online that has the potential to reach more people than flyers and billboards and commercials combined."

"For free," Crystal piped in. Maybe this was what freedom felt like.

"For free. Over time, people reading your messages will look forward to seeing your tweets and it will feel like you're old friends. This is a great place to write to anyone and make a new friend."

"Who would I write to?" Crystal was sure none of her friends used the tweeter. Other than the strange person who was already following her, no one would be waiting to hear from her.

"Anyone. Social media is an open forum where you're expected to talk to people you've never met before. If someone says something interesting about your favourite cooking show, a new kind of convection oven, or a strange new gadget, you have an open invitation to jump in on the conversation. Everyone, no matter where they live, no matter how important or unimportant they are, is allotted a voice."

"I would never do that in real life." Crystal recalled several occasions when she would have loved to jump into someone's conversation but her good sense and quiet nature prevented her from doing so.

"And now you can. Look at how other people are doing it." Brooke pointed to a tweet. "Have a look at the bakery this person is tweeting about. Type the name Cobs into the search box and see what else we can find."

Crystal's search filled the screen with messages, some written by Cobs, others written to Cobs. "Look at them all," she exclaimed, leaving fingerprints on the screen which she promptly wiped off with her apron strap.

"Look at these five in particular," Brooke said. "We can listen in on the conversation between Cobs and someone called JuneMoon.'"

Reading through the messages, Crystal was puzzled with the exchange. "Why didn't JuneMoon just call Cobs to see if they had any sourdough bread? There are faster ways to get an answer than this."

"She certainly could have telephoned them," Brooke replied. "She could have emailed them or dropped by the store too, but it looks like JuneMoon is a regular tweeter and she knew that Cobs tweets regularly too, enough for this to be a reasonable option."

"It's still weird," Crystal said. "Anyone can listen in on their conversation."

"Sometimes, as with this conversation, it doesn't matter who hears what you're talking about. Social media has become a normal way for people to interact with each other. It's no longer much different from an email or a phone call, even though a few more people may hear what you have to say. Besides, it's a nice way for Cobs to let other people know that they have sourdough bread."

"Well, if Cobs can do it, I can do it too," Crystal said. "Their tweets make me want to stop by and see what smells they've come up with. Maybe this Tweeter thing could work out for me too."

"I like seeing that smile on your face," Brooke said. "Let's try something a bit different now. Search for the word bakery and tell me about the first tweet you see."

Crystal completed the search and read the first message, puzzled at what she could possibly say about it.

 PieGal
Chris Wheaton

My bakery makes a mean apple blossom pie!

"This person likes apple blossom pie."

Brooke said not a word. She appeared to be waiting for more.

"It's good that she's likes it," Crystal said, trying to pull a confirmation out of Brooke. "That she likes the pie."

"Dig deep into the message," encouraged Brooke, nodding. "Do some free association, some introspection, some qualitative, n of 1 research. Tell me about the personality, the intentions, the opinions hiding in that message."

Crystal squinted at the message, wondering how she could possibly pull so much information out of such a short message. She read it again slowly. There had to be something more, something that Brooke clearly understood. "This person, this lady –"

"There we go," Brooke interrupted. "The first piece of information is that this is a woman's opinion. Keep going."

Crystal's face brightened and she pushed forward. "Her name is PieGal so I guess she loves pie. And she's writing about the apple blossom cake, so I guess she likes cake and apples." Crystal ran her fingers along the edge of the table to help her think. "Is that what you wanted?"

"Almost there," Brooke said. "Why does this meaningless comment about some random event in her life matter?"

Crystal stared at the message with the intensity she usually applied to icing perfect circles on her cupcakes. She jolted upright in her chair. "I got it. We care because we want to bake things that she wants to buy. She's telling the store to keep making Apple Blossom Cake. That she'll buy Apple Blossom Cake."

"That's exactly it," Brooke said. "PieGal may not have said it outright, but she just gave the store her shopping list. If they make it, she will buy it. Wouldn't you love it if your customers told you exactly what they wanted to buy?"

Crystal grinned. She could already imagine hundreds of tweets flooding in listing out exactly which brownies and tarts and cookies and cakes to bake. She could forget about painstakingly scrounging through recipe books and trying to be psychic. She could simply listen to all of the suggestions on the tweeter.

"Earth to Crystal." Brooke poked Crystal's arm. "I can tell from the silly grin on your face that something has clicked."

"I'm here, I'm here," Crystal said, with a quick shake of her head. "I was thinking about the twitters I read in the beginning. They were so stupid when I first read them, but I'm thinking they might have been more important than I realized."

"Good call," Brooke said. "Many messages seem pointless on the surface but once you dig into them, they contain an abundance of useful information. Tell me about the next message on the screen."

BestMomEver

No luck at any bakery near my work. Will anyone do a special order for 5doz pistachio cupcakes?

With a bit of practice under her belt, the dissection was quick. "This one's from a woman too. She needs a special order and she can't find anyone to do it." Crystal stopped and thought about all the time she normally spent flipping through recipe books, and trying to find new ways to make her finances work. "I can do special orders. I have the time for that."

"That's exactly what I want to hear." Brooke leaned forward in her seat and looked around the shop. "But I don't see any custom orders waiting to be picked up, I don't see any signs about custom orders, and I'm pretty sure I haven't seen any tweets from you about custom orders. Why would anyone consider asking you about special orders?"

"They will once put a sign up and tweet about it."

"I'll be watching for those," Brooke said. "Let's try one more. Tell me what this means."

SuzeBeverley
Suzanne Beverley

Thank heavens for free cookies. The bakery I always go to knows how to keep my kids quiet!

"It's another lady," Crystal began. "It seems like it's all women talking about bakeries."

"You're starting to build a theory about who your target audience is," Brooke said. "Keep that hypothesis in mind but don't fall into the trap of making generalizations from three people. Tell me what else you can take from this message."

"She's happy that her bakery gives out free cookies." Brooke turned around to look at the four dozen neatly arranged cookies in the dessert case. "Actually, I totally get that. I've had a few moms come in and they're so embarrassed when their kids run around the store screaming. I bet one single cookie would keep the kids happy."

"And the moms might have bought something in appreciation of what you did for them," Brooke said.

Crystal thought back to the leftover cookies she packed up every day, disappointed that she hadn't thought of using them as pacifiers before.

"I should have been doing that all along. The moms would have loved me," Crystal said, the words coming slowly. She sighed, thinking of the lost opportunities when moms had deserted the shop, dragging a tired and crying child behind them.

"Think positively," Brooke said. "Now you have a tool that could change everything. You're seeing the data, learning from the data, and you're figuring out how to implement your ideas."

"I thought I knew what I was doing," Crystal said. "I should have been reading this all along. I tried to figure everything out for myself and it's obvious it didn't work."

"Chin up," Brooke said. "Look here, someone has already replied to your first tweet."

"No way," Crystal exclaimed. The disappointment evaporated almost instantly as she leaned in to read it, recognizing the username as someone she'd begun to follow less than an hour ago.

 SweetPie
Linda McStorley

Welcome to Twitter, fellow baker!

"How's that for instant friendships," Brooke said. "You'll find that most people using social media are quite nice, particularly when you engage with people who have similar interests. Why don't you reply to SweetPie? Make a friend." Brooke adjusted the laptop so Crystal could type more easily. The suggestion was clearly a request.

Crystal clicked on reply and wiggled her fingers over the keys. She had so many unanswered questions and this was the perfect opportunity to get an answer. Barely a minute after typing a question, a reply from SweetPie appeared in her Twitter stream.

 SweetPie
Linda McSorley

Apple Pie, hands down, is our biggest selling item. Our customers line up for it every day

"Cool!" Crystal was thrilled with the instant advice. What if every person she followed on Twitter shared their best selling item? What if every one of them offered her one tidbit of financial advice? What if every one of them helped her with one little problem? Crystal realized what she'd been missing all along, what had been holding her bakery back. She'd been missing a mentor. And with the help of Brooke, she now had three hundred mentors.

Startled by the sound of shuffling chairs, Crystal emerged from her daydream to find Brooke gathering up her things. Crystal could barely contain her excitement. She burst out of her seat and scurried behind the counter. "Lemme pack your squares." She snatched up a flattened pie box and folded it precisely.

"You'll like these brownies. I put in twice as much chocolate as the recipe said. And I know you want some buttertarts. And these date squares are double-stuffed." Crystal tied the bursting box shut and finished it off with a bow. Crystal handed the box to Brooke who waited at the front door. "This is yours. A deal's a deal and you earned it."

Brooke opened her bookbag and laid the box on top of her books and papers. "I'll see you next week," she said, "and the week after that." Brooke opened the door and disappeared down the sidewalk.

The door creaked shut and Crystal stood alone in the bakery, plastic gloves in hand. She had sat in on one marketing class as part of her Baking and Pastry Diploma and none of this had been part of it. She had no idea who this woman was or why she wanted to help her but it didn't matter. She couldn't wait for next Tuesday.

Chapter 5

Crystal assembled the tools at her desk. She picked up the black thin-tipped Sharpie, adjusted her clear, plastic ruler by one millimetre, and applied her steady piping hand to the task. As the minutes passed, her fingers cramped under the strain and she scrunched her stress ball in and out five times. She stretched her eyes with a quick glance out the window.

An hour later, she laid the pen down for good. Crystal pestered the stress ball one last time and pronounced the job done. Given the handwritten alteration, the cards looked as good as they could. She selected a small stack of cards and placed them on top of the cash register. In tight, typewriter style printing, every business card proudly displayed Grannie's Twitter username.

Before moving on to her habitual search for the one recipe that would change everything, Crystal took one last glance out the window. A smile exploded onto her face and she burst out of her seat as the front door of Grannie's swung open welcoming the ever confident Crayon Lady.

"Guess what, guess what, guess what," Crystal called, unable to wait for Brooke to step completely into the addictive scent of oatmeal bread and sourdough buns. Brooke yanked off her scarf and crammed it into her bookbag.

"TWO people," Crystal said, her voice bursting with excitement. "TWO people came in this week and said they read one of my tweeters. TWO people." The words spewed like vanilla frosting from an icing bag left on a warm oven.

Brooke laughed. "I'm glad to see you had such a great week. You are clearly ready for your second lesson, my young padawan. Table. Laptop." With a firm gesture to the table where they'd begun their work the week before, Brooke proceeded to the back of the bakery.

Crystal grabbed her laptop and rushed to the makeshift classroom. She pulled a chair out from the table and plopped her butt down, shuffling up to the table while she waited for Brooke to remove her jacket and settle in.

"You know," Crystal said, her words coming quickly, "I wasn't so sure about you before. The first time I looked at the tweeter, it was a complete joke. And you insulted me although I don't think you knew it. But you're starting to win me over."

"Sometimes a little patience is all that's required." Brooke opened the laptop.

"I love your scarf," Crystal said. "So two people came in this week and said they saw me on the tweeter. They didn't even know my bakery was here until they saw my tweeters."

Crystal clasped her hands and tucked them under her chin. Her gigantic grin desperately needed the extra support.

"Before I fall over laughing, I need to give you a vocabulary lesson. This has got to stop." Brooke briefly covered her eyes with her hands.

"Why? What did I say?" Crystal asked, her hands dropping to her lap. She tilted her head in puzzlement.

"First, the social network we're using is called Twitter, not tweeter and not The Twitter. Second, the messages you write are called tweets not tweeters or twitters. Third, the verb is also tweet. I tweet, he tweets, she tweets, we all tweet. Got it?" Brooke looked sternly at Crystal.

"Got it. Tweets, Twits, yup." Crystal grinned.

"Alright, joker, with that out of the way, we'll continue your market researcher training," Brooke said. "From what I saw on Twitter over the last week, you've learned how and why regular people share their opinions in social media."

"You've been stalking me," Crystal teased.

"More accurately, I've been listening to your opinions," Brooke said. "Let's figure out how and why researchers collect those opinions and turn them into data that can be used for measurement and research. Research is far more than reading and acting on a few interesting tweets. Are you ready?"

"Yuppers," Crystal said. "Bring it on. Two new customers was awesome but I need a hundred new customers if I'm going to keep my shop."

"Since researchers always work with specific research objectives in mind, let's make that our objective. One hundred new customers and we'll call this project a success."

"I like it. Let's go."Crystal sat up straight and smiled wide, a perfect teacher's pet.

"Market research is how business owners, people like you, learn what consumers like and dislike about their products. Despite what you may think, we're not interested in what individual people have to say. It's not financially viable to market products and services to single people. We want to discover what motivates and interests large groups of people, hundreds of people, thousands of people."

"That's what I what. Thousands of customers." Crystal grinned and stuffed the plastic glove peeking out of her apron pocket back inside.

"We're going to focus our efforts on social media research," Brooke said, "but I'm going to explain it to you in terms of surveys because you're probably already familiar with that form of research. You've likely seen the little surveys that come with every restaurant bill or on the back of grocery receipts. You might have even seen the long census surveys that land on your doorstep every ten years when the government wants to know how many people they have to provide services for."

Crystal nodded her head. "I actually get surveys in my email every once in a while. Just a sec." She pushed her chair back a few inches and grabbed a small white plate that had been tucked behind the dessert case. She placed the oatmeal cookies on the table directly in front of Brooke. "I usually delete them -"

"Yum." Brooke's eyes immediately focused on the contents of the plate. "Why do you delete them?"

"I don't have the time," Crystal said. "They're supposed to take twenty minutes and they never do so I usually delete them. But you put a research bug in my brain and when a survey showed up in my email this morning, I figured what the heck and I answered it."

"You didn't delete it?" Brooke fingered the plate in front of her, slowly spinning it around 360 degrees.

"Not this time," Crystal answered, pleased to see the unexpected treat had done the trick. "I never pay attention to them but this one was from Wilton and I'm not particularly pleased with them right now. I bought an expensive Wilton cake pan and it warped after I used it one time. I have to prop it up with a knife to make sure my cakes come out even. As soon as I saw the survey from them, I was itching to complain." Crystal pushed the little plate a few inches closer to Brooke.

"Why wait for a survey?" Brooke asked. "Why didn't you email them or call them to explain your problem?"

"I dunno. I didn't feel like it. Besides, I don't know what address to write to. Or what I would say."

"That's too bad," Brooke said, "because they would want to hear about your experience. Do you ever tell companies about your experiences with their products? Have you shared any of your opinions on Twitter?" She pressed her finger against a crumb on the cookie plate, and tested the tiny piece of cookie for herself.

Crystal smiled. "You know the answer to that. I did say stuff on Twitter. But I didn't complain about anything. I said that my favourite pans are Williams-Sonoma. And I tweeted about my favourite vanilla beans."

"That's good news for the vanilla bean company," Brooke said. "Specialized companies selling highly targeted products have difficulties doing survey research, particularly when the few people who qualify to answer their surveys are too busy or don't care to participate. Would you have answered it?"

"Probably not," Crystal confessed. One survey over the last several years didn't work out to a very good participation rate.

"You see, there are some situations where survey research make more sense and others where social media research makes more sense. They each have unique strengths and weaknesses and you have to choose the right method for the job. With surveys, we can only listen to people who raise their hands and volunteer to respond to research surveys. We can try to convince more people to participate by offering incentives like coupons, magazine subscriptions, and gift cards, but physical incentives don't appeal to all types of people."

"You could convince me if you gave me an iPad or an iPhone," Crystal said. "That's worth twenty minutes of my time."

"You might have something there," Brooke conceded. "But, it is difficult. No matter how hard you try to convince a wide range of people to participate, only a tiny percentage of people actually will. But, social media research is a different story. The last time I checked, more than three quarters of a billion people share their opinions on a tiny social media website called Facebook-"

"You didn't say a billion?" Crystal interrupted. The crumb that Brooke had knocked onto the table was far too distracting. She must have misheard.

"You heard me correctly. Three quarters of a billion people use Facebook, half of them every single day, and two hundred million people share their opinions on Twitter. We don't even have to ask these people what their opinions are. They share their opinions every day, every hour, every minute, every second simply because they feel like chatting."

"I can't believe you said the word billion. That's like ten percent of the planet."

"Mind-boggling, I know." Brooke finally picked up a cookie. "Remember, that's just Facebook and Twitter. Imagine how many people are using social media if we include people who share their opinions on Flickr, Blogger, YouTube, Reddit and all the other thousands and millions of places where people go online to share their deepest, darkest thoughts. The online social space is far bigger than a couple of well-known websites."

"A billion," Crystal repeated. She could barely image a few hundred customers traipsing through her shop let alone a billion people using one website.

"The great thing is that with those kinds of numbers, it's possible to gather massive quantities of data and conduct a good quality social media research study. In that sense, it simply doesn't compare to surveys where you can't do the research unless you first find a large enough list of research participants. By chance, do you have the names and addresses of one thousand people who shop at your bakery?"

"You think you're so funny." Crystal pushed the cookie plate to the edge of the table furthest from Brooke. "I have nicknames for about twenty-five customers and that's it."

"Is that so," Brooke said. "What's my nickname?"

"Me to know and you to find out."

"Smart alec," Brooke said, smiling. "Let's assume you were lucky enough to have the names of one thousand people who shop at your bakery. Of the five hundred people who gave you their email address, assume three hundred of them agreed to participate. But, only seventy-five people followed through and completed your survey. Are the opinions of those seventy-five people a good representation of the original one thousand people?" Brooke broke her cookie in half and bit off the chunk with the most raisins.

"That's still a lot," Crystal said. "I'd love to have seventy-five people shopping here."

"This is a good cookie, thick and chewy," Brooke said. "From a research standpoint, seventy-five people out of one thousand people may not be good at all. For one thing, maybe the people you don't have email addresses for don't trust you enough to give you their address and would never shop here again. Or, maybe they don't have the budget for home internet which means they can't afford to shop here again. You don't know which reason it is. And what about the two hundred people who were invited to the survey but refused to participate? Maybe those people changed their minds about trusting you and they'll never shop here again. Then again, maybe they were away on holidays spending their vast fortunes and they'll be back in your shop spending lots of many any day now. You don't know."

"So I might be missing out on opinions from a group of people who either really like me or really don't like me," Crystal said.

"That's a bias that might show up," Brooke said. "Any time someone doesn't answer a survey, you have to ask why not and how does the bias impact you. Survey researchers call this the self-selection bias. Some people select themselves into surveys and other people select themselves out of surveys. It's impossible to use surveys to understand the opinions of people who don't answer surveys."

"I never realized that surveys aren't a good way to do research." Crystal took her turn eyeing the cookie plate.

"Definitely not true," Brooke said. "In fact, this is a problem for all types of market research, including social media research."

"How's that?" Crystal asked. "You just said a billion people use social media."

"Remember, not everyone has a computer at home. Not everyone has a local library where they can access the internet. And, just as you were initially fearful, not everyone feels comfortable sharing their opinions in social media. Social media research isn't perfect either."

"But these oatmeal cookies are perfect."

"That's the only reason I'm eating them," Brooke said. "Whether you use surveys or social media research, you still have to appreciate there will be biases in the data. You need to be aware of the biases if you're going to generate quality insights."

Crystal nodded her head and succumbed to temptation, picking up a cookie and nibbling away a chewy raisin from the edge.

"Let's keep thinking about our imaginary research project," Brooke continued. "Let's narrow the research focus to one product. How would you identify and gather information from people who like Challah bread?"

Crystal turned to Brooke, searching her face for a clue. "That's impossible. I can't even identify who shops at my bakery."

"I'll wait while you rethink that answer." Brooke popped a second quarter of the cookie into her mouth.

Crystal was quiet for a moment while she quickly thought about her options. Her face lit up. "Twitter," she exclaimed. "I have to search for Challah on Twitter."

Brooke brushed a few crumbs off her hands. "Congratulations on naming it properly. Surveys rely on established lists of research volunteers but when that doesn't work in your favour, Twitter is there with organic lists of target audiences. Once you search for something on Twitter, it instantly generate pages of messages from people who make, eat, want, love, and hate Challah. With social media, you don't have to spend days and weeks searching for lists of people who like or use your product because the people you are looking for identify themselves simply by naming your topic of interest. They raise their hands up like a Miley Cyrus song."

"Like a who song?"

"Not a Who song, a Miley Cyrus song."

"You've totally lost me." Crystal stared blankly at Brooke. There was a strange sense of humour in there that she had yet to figure out.

Brooke shook her head. "SMH, you need to spend more time IRL."

"What *are* you talking about?" Crystal asked. Brooke made no sense whatsoever.

Brooke leaned back in her chair and smiled. "We'll get to each of those issues later. Tell me more about the survey you took this morning. What exactly was it about?"

"I ordered a lot of equipment over the last few months and I guess Wilton wanted to know what I thought of it." I'll show them what I thought of it, Crystal mused, the crooked and nearly useless pan still weighing heavily on her mind.

"Which means they were able to take advantage of their customer list." Brooke tapped Crystal on the hand. "Online businesses are lucky because every order coming their way has a physical address and an email address attached to it. It's easy for them to do surveys because they know exactly who to talk to."

"But it was terrible," Crystal said. "I'd rather eat burnt, sugar free, fat free, gluten free muffins than answer another survey like that. I could write a survey way better." She rolled her eyes in disgust.

"Watch what you say. It seems easy but just because you can speak and write English doesn't mean you can write a survey any better than they did. When you get right down it, surveys are extremely difficult to write. Getting back to your case, what specifically was so bad about it?"

"What didn't I like? How much time do you have?" A horrified expression filled Crystal's face for an entire second before she cracked a smile.

"I hear you," Brooke said. "Perhaps you could start by telling me one thing."

Crystal dragged the sentence out as long as she could. "I could not believe how long it was. It went on and on and on like a telemarketer. It wasn't twenty minutes like they said it would be."

"Surveys shouldn't be longer than twenty minutes," Brooke said, "but one extra question turns into two extra questions and five extra questions and then it's nearly impossible to delete any of them because every one is deemed undeniably essential." Brooke began spinning the cookie plate again. She looked to be deep in thought. "There must be a way to keep surveys short, to take advantage of the best features of surveys, while still gathering opinions on a vast range of topics."

Crystal nodded her head in agreement. "I'm with you there. If surveys were shorter, a lot shorter, I might answer more of them."

Brooke finished off the last of her oatmeal cookie. She looked at Crystal, at the laptop, and then back at Crystal again. "What if you shared a few quick opinions once in a while instead of lots of opinions all at once?" she asked.

"Like tweeting," Crystal said, still nodding. She nibbled some loose crumbs from her cookie.

"There we go," Brooke said. "That's the answer I've been waiting for."

Crystal looked curiously at Brooke before finally clueing in to what she meant. Of course. Brooke didn't mean something like tweeting. Brooke *meant* tweeting.

"A one hour survey, even a twenty minute survey, is time-consuming. It's a rare person who has the time or patience to answer it, let alone the attention span and desire to do a good job of it. But, lots of people, people just like you, have the time and patience to share little tidbits of information now and then, particularly if they're in the form of fun messages to their friends."

"I've been tweeting all kinds of little things," said Crystal. "Everyone who follows me knows that I prefer the tiny chocolate chips and brown eggs, not white."

"That's exactly it," Brooke said. "Social media is a great place to share opinions about products and services you like and don't like. Some people prefer to spend ten or twenty minutes thinking about and answering a survey, while others prefer to spend a minute or two here and there sharing their thoughts in brief bursts."

"I'm on the Twitter side of things," Crystal said.

"That's coming through loud and clear," Brooke said. "Still, there's no need to choose between surveys and social media research. Sometimes, it makes more sense to use social media, sometimes surveys, and sometimes other methods we haven't even talked about. Your research objective will tell you which is the best solution."

"One hundred new customers."

"That's the plan. What else didn't you like about the survey?"

"Um, it felt like I was taking a test. I could tell there were right and wrong answers in there but I couldn't always tell what the right answer was. Actually, some of the questions were so complicated I couldn't even understand them."

"It sounds like it was an intimidating survey," Brooke said. "I'm allowed another cookie, right?"

"Each one is only about a hundred and fifty calories. Take your chances. I did feel weird answering it. The questions were so long. It was like reading something written by Shakespeare, all formal and important sounding."

"Let me take a shot at it. The questions sounded something like this." Brooke lowered her head, pondered for a moment, and then began a recitation.

"From June of last year to January of this year, have you or anyone permanently residing in your household purchased and not returned any kitchen items, including baking sheets, cake pans, small tools, or any other kitchen implements but not including major items such as stoves or fridges, from any of our Canadian or American online or brick-and-mortar outlets?"

Crystal burst out laughing, leaning so far back in her chair that it tipped and banged against the dessert case. "That's exactly it. I forgot what the question was by the time I got to the end. The answers were just as bad too. Even if I could figure out what the question meant, I couldn't always find a good answer from the list they gave. I felt like I was lying because I had to pick an answer that wasn't right."

"Sometimes, it's difficult to express your opinions accurately when you can't use your own words."

"Like I can in my tweets," Crystal said.

"You're catching on quickly," Brooke said. "When you share information and opinions in your tweets, you choose the words and ideas that make sense to you, the words that truly reflect your opinion. You can express how you feel using precise words and without being confined to little circles and checkboxes. What else didn't you like about the survey?"

"I could go on forever. Lemme think." Crystal replayed the survey in her head, skipping from one annoyance to another, finally landing on one of the major flaws. "Well, it didn't ask me about anything important."

"The survey was more than twenty minutes long and it needed to be longer?" Brooke picked up a shortbread cookie this time, a small star covered with tiny sprinkles. She broke it in half sprawling little balls all over the table.

"That's not at all what I meant." Crystal's eyes flew to the multi-coloured balls of sugar on her previously sterile table. Her hand shot out to collect them. "They asked me things I don't care about and they didn't ask me about the things I do care about."

"That can happen," Brooke said. "One of the advantages of surveys is that they can focus on specific details, often things that can't be researched any other way, rare but essential issues. In the social media space, millions of people talk about thousands of issues but they might never talk about the specific issue that the researcher is concerned with. Regardless, the survey should have provided a space for you to share any additional opinions you felt were important."

"Well, this survey missed out on the big important stuff. You know the little screws that stick out on the insides of pans? They always get caught on the spatula and they're ridiculous to clean. There wasn't anywhere on the survey to complain about that. And I have a great idea for a new kind of baking pan but they never bothered to ask. You know those pizza pans with the little holes all over? They should make professional sized baking sheets like that. Why should only French bread and pizza have a great crispy crust?"

"That's a great idea. The company should know about it," Brooke said. "They probably decided that their survey was already too long to add another question. By the way, did the survey ask you how much you agree with specific topics? Did it say something like do you strongly disagree, somewhat disagree, somewhat agree, or strongly agree with each of the following statements?"

"Those were the worst," Crystal exclaimed. "I had to answer page after page of those. I kept losing track of which row I was on. And really, what's the difference between strongly agree and somewhat agree when all I know is I agree?"

"What kind of answer would you have preferred to give?" Brooke popped the last piece of cookie in her mouth and let it melt into buttery goodness.

"Sometimes, I just wanted a yes no option and then other times I wanted to check off the spot right between strongly agree and somewhat agree. There should have been more circles, or maybe it should have let me write in my answers."

"It's a tough call," Brooke said, "deciding on how many buttons to put on a scale. Sometimes, five seems like not enough, but then seven and ten seem like too many. Perhaps your true feelings would have come through better in a tweet."

"For sure. They shouldn't have done that survey. From what you've said, they should have used social media."

"You may have answered the worst survey that was every written but social media research has its own share of problems. Surveys are perfect for measuring brand awareness but that's something that social media research can't do at all. Just because people don't talk about your shop in the social media space doesn't mean they haven't heard of it. It might mean they don't feel like talking about it, perhaps it's not relevant to them, or perhaps there isn't a location nearby."

"I guess that's a point for survey research."

"A giant point. Here's another problem. You can't use social media research to measure precise quantities or frequencies, things like how often people think about your shop, walk by your shop, come into your shop, or how much they think is acceptable to spend in your shop. Those aren't the kinds of conversations that regularly take place in social media but they are perfect in a survey."

"Another giant point?" Crystal asked.

"Definitely. Here's another one. In social media research, it's extremely difficult to identify the location of the person who is writing the message. If people in Britain are fond of pudding and people in Canada are fond of donuts and people in the US are fond of biscotti, social media won't be able to tell you that you should focus your efforts on donuts."

"That's not true at all." Crystal picked up her barely nibbled cookie and shaved a raisin off its other side. "You go to websites like Canadian Living and then you know everyone is Canadian. Easy."

"Let's test out that theory. You're Canadian. Which Canadian websites do you use a lot?"

"Well, Canadian Living."

"Name another one," Brooke said.

Crystal reached out for the cookie plate and spun it around two full turns before replying. "No fair. You put me on the spot."

"You started it," Brooke teased. "You see, that's the problem. If you think about the websites you use most often, they aren't Canadian websites, they're global websites. Twitter isn't an American or Canadian website. Facebook isn't a British or Australian website. Those are two gigantic websites that people all around the world use all the time."

"But I could use a Canadian website if I really needed to be sure I was reading Canadian opinions, right?"

"First of all, if you rarely use Canadian websites, why should anyone else? The information may not reflect a wide range of people and opinions. And second, what's to stop British or Australian people from using a Canadian website?"

"I guess nothing. But really, no one else would want to use a Canadian website. There's no reason for them to go there, don't you think?"

"That's one hypothesis. Everyone's heard of the Wall Street Journal. Do you think only Americans visit the Wall Street Journal website?"

"For sure," Crystal said. "That's an American newspaper reporting on American news so only Americans would care about it."

"Why don't we ground our theory in fact," Brooke said. "Let me show you a website called Alexa. It does a lot of background research to discover and describe the demographics of people who use specific websites, details like their age, gender, income, and region." She brought up the Wall Street Journal page on the Alexa website. "So what do you think of this where it says only fifty-five percent of their readers live in the US?"

Crystal jerked in surprise. "That can't be right," she said, examining the page more closely. "Eight percent of people are from China?"

"Basically, forty-five percent of people reading this American website don't live in the US," Brooke said. "Your hypothesis has been invalidated. Just because you know a website originates in the US doesn't mean that most of their users are Americans."

"I didn't think it would be so different," Crystal said. She was surprised to see that a local website had such interest from countries all around the world representing many different cultures and languages.

"You know, in the olden days…"

"Here we go again," Crystal said. "Bring on the ancient times."

"In the olden days," Brooke continued in a crickety old lady voice, "it was possible to control who was exposed to your marketing messages. Local newspapers were only delivered to houses in your neighbourhood, TV commercials were only shown on your local TV channel, billboards could only be viewed from the corner of Yonge and Bloor. But now, anyone can read a newspaper printed and only made available in Tokyo, Perth, or Vancouver. News spills between cities and regions and countries in the blink of an eye regardless of whether the brand managers approve."

"I can't say I've ever read a newspaper from Tokyo."

"Nor have I," Brooke continued, "but you've probably heard the news that was reported in them. Might you be interested if McDonald's issued a product recall in Ireland, or if Walmart was accused of using child labour in the Philippines? Would you care?"

"For sure," Crystal said. "I'd be mad."

"Even though it happened in another country? Even though it had no direct impact on you?" Brooke asked, once again eyeing the plate of cookies.

"I'd wanna know if they screwed up no matter where it happened. I wouldn't care if it was or wasn't the McDonald's down the street."

"Geography is a double-edged sword in the social media space," Brooke said. "We want to focus our research on opinions from specific geographical locations but we're anxious to hear news from all around the world."

"And favourite baking from around the world," Crystal said.

"If you decided that understanding the exact characteristics of people, like their age, gender, income, education, and geography, was absolutely essential, that's when you would want to use the survey method. Social media can't always provide the level of demographic detail that researchers sometimes require."

"Hey wait..." Crystal thought back to the day they'd set up her Twitter account. "Didn't I have to say I lived in Canada when I signed up for Twitter? We could use that."

"You absolutely could. Twitter does have space for people to share their geographical location, and a tiny percentage of people do indeed share it. Unfortunately, Twitter doesn't include space for any other demographic details. You would have to stalk people on multiple social networks to gather their gender from one website, their age from another, and their income and education from another. Have you got the time and inclination to do this research for thousands of people to find the few who do indeed provide it?"

Crystal waved her arm at the empty bakery. "It's either that or The Daily Bread."

Chapter 6

Crystal let out a quiet yelp of joy. After two weeks of reading and listening to tweets, paying close attention to what other bakeries were talking about, how they talked and interacted with their customers online, it was finally her turn to find success. Today, a specific Tweet caught her attention, a tweet she'd seen for other bakeries but, until now, not for her own. This precious tweet wasn't a reply and it wasn't a forward. It was simply chatter about her store.

There was only one thing to do. Crystal enlarged the text on her screen and pressed the print button. Patiently, she watched as the words jerked and jutted line by line from her printer.

MovieDaniel

Stopped by @GranniesGoodies today. Got a
delish brownie and snuck it into the lab

When Brooke arrived at the bakery for their weekly Tuesday chat, she found Crystal with a hammer in hand and a nail tucked between her lips. Crystal greeted her with a smile reminiscent of Batman's arch enemy.

"I can tell you've got news today." Brooke dropped her bookbag onto the spotless floor at their work table and joined Crystal behind the dessert case to admire a new frame taking center stage on the wall.

Crystal took the spare nail out of her mouth, releasing a gigantic grin. "Can you believe it?" She pointed madly at the lone tweet on the wall. "See this? I closed up for a few minutes this morning so I could run over to the Dollarama and buy this frame." In Barker beauty style, she swept her hands dramatically over it.

"This is the first tweet about my shop that wasn't someone tweeting back at me. I love MovieDaniel," Crystal swooned in front of the frame, pretending to kiss it.

"Congratulations," Brooke said, examining the tweet more closely. "You put a lot of work into getting that mention. I bet Daniel was happy to hear you loved his tweet so much you chose to put it on your wall."

"That's the best part," Crystal said. "I've never even talked to him. He tweeted my name out of the blue." She searched Brooke's face for a matching excited response but saw only disapproval.

F. Annie Pettit

"Why are you looking at me like that? You don't like it?" Crystal returned her gaze to the tweet, wondering if it was bragging to put it on the wall.

"I'm curious why you didn't ask Daniel for permission before you put his name on the wall for everyone to see. Were you too busy with all of your customers? Did you forget how to send a tweet to him? Maybe he quit Twitter before you could reach him?"

Caught off guard by rapid-fire questions, Crystal's mouth dropped open. "Permission for what? It was a tweet for me so I put it up. What's the problem?"

"Unfortunately, there is a problem and that is our topic of our discussion today. We need to work through issues of privacy, anonymity, and the right to determine who, what, where, when, and why you are allowed to use public information."

"Why are you making such a big deal out of this?" Crystal asked. "He mentioned my bakery on Twitter. All I did was print the tweet and put it on my wall."

"True but, unfortunately, it's not that simple. There's another party to this situation, someone you've only given cursory consideration to. Daniel Wheaton is very much involved here but you haven't considered whether he wanted his tweet framed on your wall."

"Why would he care? It's a nice tweet." Crystal smiled at the tweet, still proud of her accomplishment.

"Did you consider that maybe Daniel would be embarrassed if someone he knew saw that on your wall."

"That's silly," Crystal said. "There's nothing embarrassing about it."

62

"Are you one hundred percent positive?" Brooke asked. "How would you know what Daniel thinks is embarrassing? Let me give you an example. What if Daniel has struggled with his weight all his life, and he's been bullied and called nasty names since he was a small child. Over the last few months, he turned things around, found a good exercise program, a healthy eating pattern, and he's shared his new-found success with his friends and family."

"He's got lots to be proud of. It's all good." Crystal struggled to find the angle in Brooke's story.

"Let me finish. On that fateful day, Daniel found out he failed a college exam and he consoled himself with a brownie. But, immediately after hitting the enter key, he realized he made a mistake. He was embarrassed about his behaviour and tried to delete the tweet but Twitter wouldn't allow it. Now, thanks to you, people who don't follow him, don't read Twitter, and don't even know about Twitter can read on your wall about his lapse. His girlfriend is furious with him for giving in to such a small temptation. His mother tells him he's a failure. Our dear friend Daniel is horribly embarrassed and ashamed."

"First of all, you've gone way over board with that story," Crystal said, shaking her head. "Second of all, I'm not responsible for his mistake."

"True on both counts. The tiny slip on his diet was completely his fault. But he never asked you to print the tweet, he never requested that you frame it, and he never told you to put a spotlight on it by hanging it on a public wall in your bakery where people who don't even know about Twitter can see it."

"I guess he didn't." Crystal lowered her eyes. Her neck felt warm.

"That scenario was only to demonstrate that you could cause him embarrassment," Brooke said. "The embarrassment would be completely your fault. What about a scenario where putting that tweet in a public place endangers his life?"

"You managed to make me feel bad and you're telling me I should feel worse? How could that story get any worse?"

"I'll continue then. Our new friend Daniel, having been bullied his entire life, has disappointed his girlfriend and his mother. From his perspective, there's only one option left and that is ending his life."

"Because of a tweet." Crystal had a hard time believing that something as small as a tweet could cause so much trouble. But then, she could think of a few occasions where tiny things had embarrassed her in front of people, things she'd regretted doing.

"Sometimes, comments have more context to them than you realize. My story might be an unreasonable, made-up story, and perhaps it is highly implausible, but the only person who would know that is Dan."

Crystal stared at the picture frame and slowly unhooked it from the nail. "I get that different people are embarrassed by different things but I still think you took it too far."

"Perhaps you're right. Scratch that. Let me give you a scenario that actually happened," Brooke said. "A global pharmaceutical company worth billions of dollars visited a social network for cancer patients and copied out people's names, their embarrassing symptoms, their feelings of shame, depression, anger, and frustration, and included that information in their official research reports. In a blunder, the patients' health information was released to the public and individual people were humiliated."

"How could that happen?" Crystal asked, horrified. "What if they didn't want other people to know they had cancer?"

"Unfortunately, not everyone takes the time, like we are doing, to think about when it's appropriate to reveal people's names and their personal details."

Crystal held the picture in her hands and stared at the kind words. "What if I cover up his name so no one knows who said this?" She put the picture on the counter and pried the cardboard off the back of the frame.

"That's a step in the right direction," Brooke said, "but you'd also have to hide his avatar and his username. Those are also pieces of information that could identify him."

"But if I do that, I'll be left with just showing the tweet. That's pretty boring."

"I hate to disappoint you again, but you shouldn't show the tweet either," Brooke said. "Even if you hide his username and his real name, I could still tell you exactly who wrote it."

"How's that? Are you psychic?" Crystal pulled a pen and pad of paper out of her apron pocket and made a big show out of preparing to record a prediction. "What am I planning to bake tomorrow?"

"If only I was psychic." Brooke picked up the frame, took Crystal's arm and guided her to the table that Crystal had readied with the laptop. "Sit down. I want you to try something. Go to your Twitter profile and find a tweet from yesterday, preferably one that could be taken out of context by a careless reader. Paste part of your tweet into Google and show me the results."

Crystal picked through her Twitter stream and chose an appropriate tweet. The search result appeared. She instantly felt all the air rush out of her lungs and the blood drain from her face. How could this be?

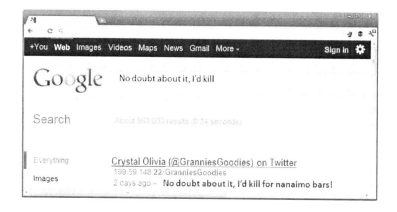

"No way." She turned to Brooke, shock enveloping her face. "I'm the first result. Me. And it looks like I'd kill someone when that's not what I said at all. How did Google find me? This is... scary."

"Absolutely, you might forget to put baking soda in your cookies once in a while but Google's all powerful database never forgets anything, no matter how long ago it happened, no matter how tiny or embarrassing it was. Ever. Even if you think you are being nice by removing someone's name and identifying information from their message, you will not have accomplished what you set out to do."

Crystal continued to stare at the Google result. This was more Big Brother than she had ever thought. This was why Brooke was so firm in her opinions about privacy. This was creepy.

"Earth to Crystal," Brooke called, poking her on the forearm. "Let's keep going. We aren't out of options yet."

Crystal yanked her gaze away from the screen. "What should I do?"

Brooke leaned back in her chair. "One option is to adjust the words a little bit. Switch a couple of the words to synonyms in the same style, choose different slang, different acronyms, make words plural instead of singular, make it future tense instead of past tense, switch a spelling mistake from one word to another. Make enough small changes so that the essence of the original message remains but a search engine like Google or Bing can't instantly locate it. It's not perfect, but it will be impossible for the average person to identify the author."

"If I can't show anything I should just tweet a message to myself and frame that." Crystal frowned. She didn't like seeing her options slowly being eliminated one by one.

"Fortunately, you still have one unexplored alternative at your disposal."

Crystal's face brightened. "What, what is it?"

"Send him a private message on Twitter and ask for permission. If he doesn't respond to you, then the answer is no."

"Sheesh, I could have avoided this whole conversation by asking for permission first?" Crystal grinned at Brooke and reached for the frame, popping the piece of cardboard back into it. "Well, that I can do. I'll hang this in the kitchen until MovieDaniel gives me permission to put it up here."

"Perfect. You can still be proud of it there. By the way, will there be any cookies today?" Brooke tried to peer around the counter but a thoughtfully prepared plate was not in plain view.

Crystal grinned. "You have a sweet tooth like I do." She leaned back in her chair and rummaged around behind the counter until her fingers touched something. She pulled out a plate of gooey double-fudge brownies and put them immediately in front of Brooke.

"You are nasty." Brooke reached out to position the plate, spinning it around and admiring the brownies from all sides. "I knew I smelled something fabulous when I walked in today. When people do find your bakery, your sales will go through the roof."

"I hope so," Crystal said. "I still have a question. Why do people write things online if having someone read it would embarrass them?"

"Deserves a simple answer, doesn't it," Brooke said. "If you leave a written conversation on the internet, which is public, then technically anyone can pay attention to it. In the same vein, we're sitting here having a public conversation and the masses of people wandering through your bakery could also listen in if they felt like it."

"I'm liking the masses." Crystal nodded her approval of the story.

"I thought you would. What if you and I were chatting about a bunch of different things and you told me your doctor was worried about your stress levels. What if a stranger broke away from the crowd I see over there at the brownie case and stood right here in our personal space, listening to every word. What if he took notes?"

"I like the part about the crowd at the brownie case but I don't like the weirdo. I'd tell him to bug off."

"Smart move. Weirdo moves away as instructed," Brooke directed. "Before he leaves your shop though, he goes over to the front window where all your bills are openly displayed on your desk, and he copies down your name, your email address, and your home address."

"My creep-o-meter just went off again."

"How is that possible?" Brooke asked, an exaggerated look of shock on her face. "Are you telling me that you expect privacy even though your bakery is a public place?"

"Oh, that was sneaky." Crystal shook her finger at Brooke. "I see what you're getting at."

"In traditional opinion research, privacy is built into the process with permission forms that ensure an appropriate level of respect and privacy is maintained."

"That's how I can complain on a survey and no one knows it was me."

"And you can feel safe sharing your honest opinions even if they might be embarrassing," Brooke said. "In the social media space, there are no forms or privacy agreements but that doesn't matter. Many people still feel like they have personal space on the internet and that only certain people are allowed in it. We say things on Twitter for our two hundred followers to listen to and we say things on our blogs for our twelve readers to appreciate. We know we're saying or writing things in public places, but we still feel like and expect to have a bit of privacy within the confines of how we use that public space."

"I'm still creeped out by this tweet."

"Let me go back to permissions and passwords then, something that many websites require."

"Like Facebox."

"Oh, that hurt."

Pleased with herself, Crystal crossed her arms and grinned.

"Some websites let you read and look at their contents any time you want and all of the information shows up in search engines. But, if you want to comment on something or engage with other people on the site, you have to create a password so other people will know who made the comment. The password is essentially a tracking device and it takes only a few seconds for anyone to get one."

Crystal pushed the brownies closer to Brooke, trying to catch her off guard. But the move was to no avail and Brooke continued without hesitation.

"But then, other websites won't let you see anything until after you sign up and create a password. Search engines may want to show you the contents of the website but they can't because their programming won't permit it. The website is still accessible but you have to take a minute to create a password before you can go inside and read or comment on anything."

"I've been on both kinds of those websites," Crystal said. "I like the ones where you can see everything without creating passwords. It's easier."

"In the baking space, passwords for personal protection are probably inconsequential. But let's go back to the story of our unfortunate friends dealing with cancer. They found a password protected website created specifically for cancer patients to share their thoughts and opinions in a safe place. They could talk about their embarrassing symptoms, and feel safe and respected no matter how difficult their lives."

"It's good that there are websites like that," Crystal said. "I'd want a place to talk privately with other people who understood me."

"It's also a website that you could take advantage of right now," Brooke said. "You could use the cancer patient social network to grow your business."

"How's that?" Crystal tilted her head in puzzlement.

"Don't forget, cancer patients are regular people like you. They go to work, raise families, and eat and drink. When they're on the patient website, they probably talk about their unique dietary requirements, the foods that do and don't make them nauseous and, are you listening, the bakeries that do and don't accommodate those special needs."

Crystal's ears had perked up as soon as Brooke said the word food and ideas were already percolating. "I could be the bakery that caters to cancer patients. Is that a real website? Can we look at it?"

"There's the problem." Brooke held out her hands in a mock stop sign. "Did you forget that the website is password protected? They're using that password to keep embarrassing information in and unwanted people out. Are you an unwanted person?"

"What?" Crystal was surprised at the question. She certainly wasn't a giant corporation taking advantage of unfortunate people. "Of course, I'm not. I'm a nice regular person."

"Do you have cancer? Are you dealing with chemotherapy? Radiation? Are you throwing up constantly? How are you a wanted person on that website?"

She felt like she'd been punched, each question more painful than the last. "I don't have cancer but I wouldn't do anything," Crystal said. "I'd listen quietly. Besides, if anyone can get a password, what's wrong me poking around?"

"Even if it takes only a few seconds to get a password, that password still means something," Brooke said. "It's a request for privacy, a notice that the people inside the walls want to be left to themselves. It's essentially a sign on their door that say please don't put our information out there for the public to see."

"I guess you're right. But I'd still want to have a peak and learn about the problems they're having with food," Crystal said.

"And that might be fine. But don't bother the people, don't copy out their information, and definitely do not record their names. Just listen, learn, and respect their privacy."

"So that nothing embarrassing gets out," Crystal said.

"The ideal scenario is that nothing embarrassing gets out, but more importantly that no identifying information gets out," Brooke said. "But we know the risks all too well. Software corrupts, ill-intentioned people hack into websites, little bits and pieces of software and hardware malfunction all the time. Private information can become public at the drop of a hat."

"That would never actually happen," Crystal said. "Companies spend a ton of money to make sure it doesn't happen." At least, she assumed they did.

"Unfortunately, the worst case scenario has happened over and over in the last couple of years. Databases containing thousands and millions of financial and medical records have been hacked, lost, or accidentally or wilfully leaked on the internet. There is only one solution. If you are ever concerned about something being in the public space, never write it on the internet. In fact, never write it down and never speak it aloud. If you put information on a website, on a social network, you must assume it is public information. Most Ts&Cs say exactly that."

"Teas and sees?"

"My apologies for the annoying acronym." Brooke smiled and shook her head. "Most websites have a horribly long and painful Terms and Conditions document, the T&C that you must read before you're allowed to use the website."

"I've never read one," Crystal said, curious how she could have missed an important document. "I don't think I've ever seen one."

"Then you're like ninety-five percent of people using the internet. Usually when you sign up for a website, there's a tiny little box you have to check off that says something like '*I have read and agreed to the terms and conditions of this website.*' Does that sound familiar?"

Crystal crinkled her eyes and thought for a moment. "Maybe but I'm sure I've never read one."

"They're usually written in overly complicated legal language that the regular person can't possibly understand. Those documents are where you'll find statements like *We may share all of your information including your name, photos, and personal details with third-party vendors* and Twitter even says something like *what you say on Twitter may be viewed all around the world instantly.*"

Crystal stared intently at Brooke, trying to piece together everything she had learned. "So I'm back to my same question. Why are you making such a fuss about MovieDaniel when he had to check that box too?"

"Is that your lead argument? If something isn't illegal, it's fair game?"

"Sure, why not." Crystal shrugged her shoulders. She had no idea what to think now. The arguments for both view points were equally strong.

"What a wonderful world. That would mean there is no need to hold doors open for people, return lost items, let a disabled person have your seat on the bus, or help people pick up their dropped packages. It's self-centered and rude, but as you say, it's not illegal."

Crystal frowned. Brooke had a good point. "That's not what I meant at all though."

"You know Crystal, it has to come back to thinking about the other person. *You* know that the internet is completely public but many people don't truly understand the extent of public. People know that their five or ten friends are listening to them but it doesn't occur to them that other people, let alone global corporations, are listening as well."

"They should read the Tees and Cees. Like they're supposed to." Crystal wondered if she should start her own Bingo card with all the words that kept getting repeated and all the strange new words she was learning. Listen would definitely be one of those words.

"I hope they do," Brooke said. "But until we know that most people actually do read and understand them, we can't penalize people for being ill-informed. The strong shouldn't prey on the weak."

Brooke picked up two brownies in one hand and grabbed her bag with the other. "Work through that conundrum. I have class."

Crystal dropped her chin on her hands and stared at the computer. Her brain was a jumble of ethical dilemmas.

Chapter 7

Crystal prepared her first scientific experiment. Over the last few days, she'd come across four messages from four different people chatting about bringing home hot buttered tea biscuits from their bakery every weekend. With that secret intelligence, Crystal spent two afternoons scouring her books and tweaking what was certain to become Grannie's one of a kind, prize-winning tea biscuit recipe.

Saturday was newly christened as tea biscuit day and three dozen English tea biscuits were glazed with buttermilk and baked to a crispy golden brown. Set to cool on the dessert case, the aroma wafted through the bakery, severely testing Crystal's will. The experiment was completed when she hit the enter key on her laptop.

GranniesGoodies
Crystal Dillis

Hot tea biscuits directly out of the oven, you know you love them

In keeping with her newly devised social media strategy, Crystal waited a couple of hours before tweeting to her Twitter followers that strawberry jam was a perfect accompaniment for tea biscuits. At noon, she tweeted that tea biscuits are a tasty quick snack before lunch. When closing time finally came, she didn't tweet. She simply packed up the tea biscuits, minus the one she'd sold and the two she'd eaten herself, and grudgingly labelled the box with a Sharpie.

When Tuesday arrived, Crystal's growing frustrations were to blame for forgotten ingredients, lost recipes, and burnt edges. She'd done everything right. She'd followed the right people, tweeted and listened to tweets, and carefully dissected every tweet to make sure she knew exactly what people were talking about. She'd sold one tea biscuit.

"Listen to people and they'll tell you what they want," Crystal announced to the empty bakery, her arms outstretched. She yanked open the glass door on the brownie case, shifted a tray two millimetres to the left and slammed the door closed. "I'll tell YOU what they want–."

As the door creaked open announcing Brooke's arrival, Crystal clapped her hand over her mouth. Her outburst had been overheard.

"Hi there, sunshine." Brooke loosened her scarf from her neck.

Crystal stood motionless, red-faced. "Hi, nothing." She didn't bother with the cheerful shopkeeper facade.

Brooke eased up to the counter. "Embarrassed in a public place, are you? It looks like you've had a difficult week. Come. Classroom time." Quietly, gently, she gestured at Crystal to follow her.

Dragging her heels, Crystal picked up the laptop and slogged to the back table. She dumped the laptop onto the table and immediately began to spew.

"My research said that people like tea biscuits on Saturday morning so I made tea biscuits on Saturday morning. Know how many I sold? One. One measly tea biscuit." Crystal slumped in her chair like a defiant child refusing to eat a bowl of horrible stewed rhubarb.

"That's unfortunate," Brooke said. "You've had some success with social media and this week did not build on that momentum."

Crystal stared at the table. She noticed the deep scratch she'd spent hours trying to sand away was still obvious. It looked like a mushroom.

Brooke continued. "I understand you need to see improvements in your business or you won't have a business at all. I know that. I need you to trust me. I'm going to do my best to help you, OK?" Brooke spoke slowly, her voice clear and strong.

Crystal's nod was barely perceptible. The mushroom scratch was far easier to pay attention to. Maybe if she sanded it a little bit more, the flaw wouldn't be so noticeable.

"You said you tweeted with a lot of people to find out what to bake."

Crystal broke her silence. "Yup." She tilted her head and noticed that, from an angle, the mushroom scratch almost looked like a little girl wearing a floppy sunhat.

"Twitter is one social media website among millions where people like to share their opinions. So far, it's the only place where I've shown you how to listen to other people's opinions."

Crystal shifted her attention from the mushroom to the scuff running the full length of her sneaker. "And…"

"Let me put this in food terms." Brooke pointed to the dessert case where the cookies were displayed. "Tell me about the people who spend most of their time in front of the cookie case, the people who buy your cookies."

Finally paying attention, Crystal responded. "Um, it's mostly moms and kids. I constantly have to wipe nose and fingerprints off the glass. That's why the Windex is right there."

Pointing to the middle dessert case, Brooke asked her question again. "Who buys the squares?"

In her mind, Crystal pictured the few people who had been sweet enough to buy an entire box of squares. "Lots of people, but it's usually women bringing squares to dinner parties I think. Like a hostess gift."

"And who buys the tarts and brownies in the front case?"

"I wouldn't say there's any one group of people for those. It's lots of different people. What does this have to do with my tea biscuits?"

"Let me switch things up again, Crystal. What are your favourite websites?"

"I like the Jamie Oliver website and the Martha Steward website. They have really interesting recipes."

"What other websites? Where else do you go online?"

"Sometimes, I go to Flickr," Crystal said. "The photographs are delicious and I get lots of decoration ideas. I like YouTube because I can watch videos of people handling the piping bag."

"In other words, when you feel like looking for recipes, you go to one website and when you feel like looking at pictures, you go to another website. You have a different reason to visit each website."

Sensing an intriguing revelation, Crystal leaned forward. "Yeah. I do different things on different websites."

"Now tell me, how are your dessert cases similar to your websites?" Brooke asked.

Crystal fidgeted in her chair and considered each of the dessert cases. "People like different things. Some people prefer to eat squares and look at Flickr. Other people prefer to eat cookies and look at YouTube. Is that it?" She turned to face Brooke, a quizzical look on her face.

"You've almost figured out the problem with your tea biscuit research," Brooke said. "When you listened to the people on Twitter, you only listened to people who like to chat on Twitter and you completely ignored people who prefer to chat on Flickr or YouTube. You didn't listen to the entire population of people talking about bakeries."

"But I read so many tweets," Crystal said, exasperated. "I read hundreds of them. I probably read thousands of them."

"Sometimes, more isn't better. Sometimes, more is simply more misleading. Think about this. You said yourself that you to go to different websites for different reasons and that's a reflection of your personality, the kind of person you are. Well, some people like to share their opinions in bits of easily digestible knowledge, like quick chats, short messages, and fun tweets. Other people prefer to share their opinions in well-thought out blogs, comments, or reviews. And then, of course, there is a completely different group of people who comment on YouTube videos of cats playing the piano. Those three different kinds of people use three different parts of the internet, right?"

"I guess so," Crystal said, "but I'm still waiting." She wondered if the cat could actually play the piano.

"Here is the answer. The reason your tea biscuits were a disaster is that you only listened to opinions from people who like to chat on Twitter, people who represent only fifteen percent of the internet population, the keeners, the early adopters, the people who like quick and short. You based your decision to bake tea biscuits on listening to a sample of people who do not reflect the average person."

It finally sunk in. "I listened to weird people," said Crystal.

"A couple years ago, you might have been able to say that, but not anymore. The people on Twitter aren't weird, but their opinions are often different from those you'd find elsewhere. There's a famous story that every introductory research class learns about. The basic story is this. Once upon a time…" Brooke drew the words out long for the full effect.

"Get on with it." Crystal feigned a yawn.

"In 1936, a magazine called Literary Digest surveyed two million Americans. They generated a massive sample size by gathering contact information from telephone books and vehicle registration logs. There were 128 million people in the US at that time so to create a list of two million was a stunning accomplishment. This large sample size allowed them to predict who the next president of the United States would be. Tell me, who did they predict?"

"1936, 1936." Crystal closed her eyes and thought back a few years to her high school history classes. It wasn't her best class, but she'd always been a good student. "That's Roosevelt, right?"

"Is that your final answer?" Brooke asked.

"Yup."

"I'm sorry to tell you you're wrong. Franklin Roosevelt was indeed the president of the United States in 1936 but the Literary Digest predicted a massive win by Alf Landon."

"I guess they didn't survey enough people," Crystal said.

"That's one possibility," Brooke said, "but the sample size was not the problem. These days, researchers do most of their political polls with samples of a few thousand people, even samples of a few hundred people, and their predictions are reasonably accurate. So tell me, how can researchers today do a good job with two thousand people when the Literary Digest did a horrible job with two million people?"

"A really bad survey?"

Brooke chuckled. "That's something you have experience with. There are probably one or two less than perfect surveys out there. But think back to 1936, when your Grannie was a young lady. Who owned cars and telephones?"

"Two million people did," Crystal said. "That's a lot of people."

"Except that in 1936, those were two million wealthy people. The person who ran that presidential prediction survey based their work on the voting preferences of the two million wealthiest people in the country. Since Roosevelt was well-known for being a president of the people, not the wealthy minority, the problem with the survey was that it didn't listen to a representative group of people."

"So their prediction was wrong because they only surveyed rich people."

"That's it," Brooke said. "Just as you only listened to a specific type of conversation, they only listened to a specific social-economic status. They surveyed wealthy people, you listened to keeners with short attention spans. That, my dear, was your big mistake."

Crystal leaned back in her chair and closed her eyes. An entire week wasted and one week closer to bankruptcy.

Chapter 8

"How do I fix it?" Crystal wasn't about to give up now, just when this Twitter thing was starting to make sense. She had to keep pushing.

"You need to listen to everyone on the internet, not just a specific segment of the internet, and I'm going to show you how to do that. After today, you'll be able to listen to people no matter what part of the internet they prefer using. You're going to do your research using the ultimate search engine. You're going to use Internet Explorer."

"Done and done," Crystal replied, relieved to hear a solution was at hand. She typed Internet Explorer into her browser.

Brooke burst out laughing. "Stop that travesty, I'm kidding." She pushed Crystal's hand away from the keyboard. "Search for Google Alerts. That's what you want."

Crystal clicked to the website and read the page. "What does it do?" she asked.

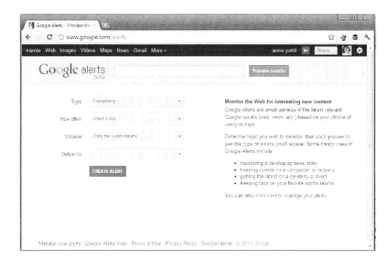

Crystal leaned back in her seat, careful not to tip it over, and grabbed the plate she'd tucked behind the counter. Two fat buttertarts filled it nicely.

Temporarily distracted by the pecans sticking out of sugary goodness, Brooke continued. "Google Alerts is a tool that sends you emails according to your specifications. If your favourite musician is Katy Perry, you could tell Google Alerts to send you an email every time she is mentioned on the internet. As soon as she announces a show, or a press release comes out, or a blog post is written about her, an email will show up in your inbox telling you about it. It will only send you a small sample of what's available but chances are you'll know the instant she kisses a girl."

"Who cares if she kisses a girl." Completely uninterested in a stranger's preferences, Crystal poised her fingers at the keyboard, awaiting further instructions.

"Perhaps no one. Why don't we instead ask Google Alerts to send you an email if someone mentions your bakery? Google Alerts will stay on top of any blog posts or reviews or comments about Grannie's that come along."

"I can speed this up a bunch," Crystal said. "No one's saying anything about Grannie's so Google won't send me any emails."

"Perhaps right now, but if you keep up your Twitter work, Google Alerts will surprise you. All you need is a bit of patience, my dear."

"Easy for you to say. My bank account says I have about three weeks of patience left."

"That's a tight deadline so get typing. Make an Alert for Grannie's Goodies and make sure to spell it wrong."

"I know how to spell the name of my own bakery." Crystal turned to Brooke, curious about the odd request. "Do you?"

"It doesn't matter if you or I can spell. What matters is whether other people can spell. You know, not everyone is a spelling bee champion and you want to hear opinions from all types of people even if they're bad spellers, lazy spellers, or people who are still learning English. And even then, you have to account for people standing on crowded buses who are hanging on to the safety bar with one hand and trying to hit tiny little buttons on their iPhone with the other hand while the bus unexpectedly starts and stops. Finally, my favourite reason for making sure you include misspellings is that you have to account for people who have a sense of humour."

"I was following you right up until the sense of humour," Crystal said. "What does humour have to do with anything?"

"I think it's time for a word game. Give me a slang word for Walmart that everyone knows actually means Walmart."

"You mean with the dash or the star in the middle?"

"Not quite. I'll give you one for free. As a term of endearment, some people like to say wallyworld instead of Walmart. Give me another name for Walmart."

Crystal pondered for a moment before giving up. "I can't even guess."

"If you weren't particularly fond of Walmart, you might find it humorous to call it walbarf, right?"

Crystal slapped her hand over her mouth and laughed. "I've never heard that."

"I've heard it too many times. There are other popular slang terms as well, like walfart and walmartian. The point is that if we don't think about gathering opinions that use the slang words, our research results could turn out to be more positive than they should be."

"Walmart is just unlucky."

"They aren't the only ones. It's a widespread problem," Brooke said. "How many ways can you spell Starbucks without using the correct spelling?"

Crystal traced her finger over the mushroom scratch on the table. "How about starbox?"

"And..."

"Starbuks without the c?"

"Those are much better guesses than your Walmart guesses. There's also sbucks, fourbucks, and, of course, two very popular, very negative, very inappropriate slang words."

"Tell me, tell me. You can't say that and not tell me." Crystal's eyes opened wide and she waited eagerly to hear more new slang.

"If you don't mind a little nastiness, try replacing the b with either an s or an f. Those options may not be officially or politically correct, or even sanctioned by the brand, but people use them to refer to the brand and that makes them important to include. If you listen to everyone's opinion, no matter how they spell your brand name, you'll collect the most comprehensive and truthful set of data."

Still smiling about her growing vocabulary, Crystal set up a Google Alert to catch as many misspellings and alternate spellings for her bakery as possible. She included GrannysGoodys, GranniesGoodies, GranniesGoodys and GrannysGoodies. And, she was careful to also include versions with spaces and without, as well as with dashes and without, to account for opinions from people who weren't sure how to refer to her shop.

"Let's do a few more," Brooke said. "Set up alerts for a few of the bakeries you're following on Twitter so you can learn what people are saying about them across the internet."

Brooke watched as Crystal set up an alert from a specialty pie shop simply and elegantly called Apple Pie. "Are you sure that's a bakery you want to keep track of?" Brooke asked.

"Absodefinitely," Crystal said. "The pictures they put on Twitter make me want to lick the screen. If I ever start selling pies, those are the pies I want to copy."

"I can appreciate that," Brooke said. "You've tweeted a few pictures that made me want to do the same. There's a problem though. Use the phrase Apple Pie in a sentence but don't use it to refer to that bakery."

"Easy," Crystal exclaimed, preparing to impress Brooke with a quick as a wink answer. "My mom makes apple pie.'" Her hands dropped to her lap. "Oh, no."

"If it's that easy for you to use the phrase in a way that doesn't mean the bakery, think about how often thousands and millions of other people will do the same thing. Chances are that 99.99 percent of the Alerts for apple pie will have nothing to do with the bakery and everything to do with mom's home baking."

"I guess I can't do that one," Crystal said, disappointed. "Shoot."

"It's a common problem," Brooke said. "If you liked the spelling quiz, I've got another quiz for you. Ready?"

"Always," Crystal said.

"Alright, imagine you own a multi-million dollar chain of clothing stores and you sell clothing for men, women, and children all around the world. You'd like to track social media opinions about your store so you search online for mentions of your brand name. For argument's sake, let's say the store is Target. Use the word target in a sentence but don't refer to the store."

Crystal pushed the plate of buttertarts closer to Brooke and spun it a little. "Aim for the target?"

"My turn. I hit my sales target last quarter." Brooke picked up a buttertart and gazed at it from all sides.

"I went to target practice but I forgot to bring my bow and arrow." Crystal grinned, pleased with her creative answer.

"I didn't know you had any time for archery," Brooke said. "Let's stay with the clothing store theme. Use the word Gap in sentence but make sure you don't refer to the store."

Crystal picked up a buttertart for herself and nibbled at the edge of the pastry. "Got it. Madonna has a gap between her teeth. Yeah, I know something about popular music."

"That's still to be debated," Brooke said. "But I do think you understand the problem. Just like Gap and Target, many brand names have double and triple meanings. Insurance companies like Nationwide and Progressive, and car rental companies like Hertz and Enterprise suffer from the same problem of generic brand names. Any data for them could be massively contaminated with irrelevant data if there isn't a detailed process for removing the wrong pieces of data."

"That's why I'm not setting up an Alert for Apple Pie," Crystal said. "I don't want to spend all my time deleting the wrong ones."

Brooke nodded. "Here's a similar problem. What if you wanted to research what consumers think about high-fructose corn syrup?"

"I don't bake with that so I'm not worried," Crystal said. "But there can't possibly be a double meaning for a word that long."

"I agree with you there. There are far too many letters in that word. It would far easier to say and spell if we call it HFCS but that's when we do find double meanings." Brooke bit into her buttertart, the sugary goo dripping onto her fingers.

"For HFCS? What else could possibly use the same letters?"Crystal asked, trying to think of anything that might use a remotely similar acronym.

Brooke licked the goo from her fingers. "Hydrofleurocarbons."

"Hydro what?" Crystal asked, not even attempting to stumble over a word no one should know.

"Holy Family Catholic School," Brooke said. "Wait. No. Houston Friendship Center Society. Hoosiers For a Conservative Senate. Housing, Food, and Conference Services. Oh, and hydrofleurocarbons. Those are all real. Do you want more?"

Crystal laughed. "I get it, I get it. I never would've thought that a weird acronym could have so many meanings."

"It's another case of thinking outside the bakery. Do you ever wonder how your diet affects your blood pressure? You could do some interesting research on BP, don't you think?"

"You're telling me that BP stands for something else, right?"

"Since it's only two letters, BP is even worse than HFCS. Acronyms are your friend when you want to make sure you've got every important piece of data but they are also a vicious enemy. Find me a website called the Acronym Finder website and tell me what BP stands for."

After a quick search, Crystal read through the results on the website.

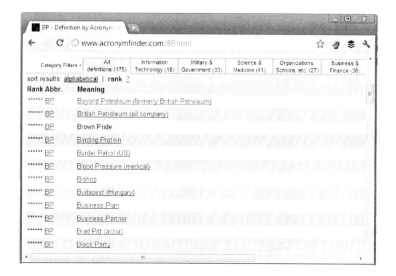

"Oh wow, I almost forgot that BP oil spill from a few years ago. No one said British Petroleum. They always said BP."

"Which means that anyone researching that company would have to be careful," Brooke said. "Their BP data could be full of data about blood pressure, basis points, Boston Pizza, Border Patrol, business plans, boiling points, and more. You see, every acronym, no matter how unique you think it is, has at least five doppelgangers. You have to expect them, search for them, get rid of them and then you'll have beautiful, clean data."

"Do you think Grannie's has a doppelganger?" Crystal nibbled further around the edge of her buttertart.

"Possibly," Brooke said. "Fortunately, Grannie's Goodies isn't a phrase that people use in their everyday language unless they are specifically referring to your shop. There will probably be a few errors here and there but your brand name has a base level of data validity and quality built right into it."

"That was my plan all along," Crystal said. At least, she thought, now that she knew it could have been a problem.

"Of course it was. It's certainly a lesson for people who work in branding. Now that social media is such a major part of our lives, anyone who names a product or service or store must be extremely careful to choose an easily and uniquely searchable name. Like the name of your shop."

"Thank you, thank you. I accept all compliments." Crystal attempted a low bow in her chair.

"You're welcome," Brooke said. "Professional software would be able to pick apart the Apple Pie bakery from mom's apple pie, but most people doing research on their own, like you, have to make some concessions regarding data quality. Google Alerts won't give you professional level quality but sometimes you have to use whatever is available."

"It's still better than only looking at Twitter, right?"

"You've got it," Brooke said. "Set up a few more alerts so you can track your competitive bakeries and be sure to set up something for bakeries in general. Many people won't mention a specific bakery, but they will talk about bakeries in passing and that, too, is important information."

"That's a lot of Alerts," Crystal said. "But I'm on it." On it like Brooke on that buttertart, she thought.

"Watch your email box," Brooke said. "You'll start to receive some detailed category and competitive information. You might not get any emails about your shop right away but don't let that concern you. Your business isn't the only one not being mentioned in social media."

"Like the mani-pedi shop next door," Crystal joked.

"Watch what you say. Just because that shop is closed doesn't mean it isn't generating online chatter. There could be a number of people complaining about how it makes the neighbourhood look run down."

"I'd be happy if it was a cute little pet shop that brought in lots of customers. Then those customers would come to my bakery too."

"Lots of customers would be good, but it won't guarantee lots of social media data. There are thousands of companies out there, far bigger than you, companies that earn billions of dollars, that rarely get talked about in the social media space."

Crystal dropped her hands to the table in surprise. "How's that possible? Like who?"

"Are you familiar with the Fortune 500 list? It's a ranking of US companies that bring in enormous revenues, companies like Walmart, Exxon, and Chevron. But have you heard of McKesson, Valero, Wellpoint, or Hess?"

"Nope, never."

"Exactly my point. It doesn't matter how many customers you have or how big your company is. If you aren't selling products and services that regular people want to talk to their friends about, you won't be able to take advantage of all of the benefits of social media research. Only brands that inspire people to talk about them, whether good or bad, can use social media research to learn about their own brand perceptions. You, on the other hand, are in a good position. Maybe no one is talking about you today, but if you play your cards right, a lot of people will be talking about you in a few weeks, a few months."

"If I'm still here."

"I do believe you're teasing me with that negativity. There may not be any status updates or comments about your bakery right now, but you can learn a lot from what people say about other bakeries."

"I'm already getting tons of ideas from the other bakeries on Twitter."

"I knew there was a researcher in you," Brooke said. "When the Alerts start flowing in, you'll get information from many more sources than Twitter and you'll need to organize all of that information, all those emails, in a useful way, in an Excel spreadsheet."

"No problem. I use Excel all the time for my finances. My lack of finances." Crystal sighed.

"Glad to hear it because we'll need every bit of skill you have," Brooke said. "I want you to break down every email into its components. Copy the date in one column, the author into one column, the message in another, and so on for every piece of information you can find in each email."

"Easy," Crystal said. "Balancing my finances, not so easy."

"That's step one. What I'm far more interested in is step two, something called Content Analysis."

"No problemo," Crystal said. "I have no clue what that is but I know I can do it."

"That's good to hear," Brooke said. "Content analysis is a qualitative research method used to categorize the contents of written text and in our case, messages written in the online space."

"Categorize them into what?" Crystal asked. From what she'd just heard, it sounded like she'd done content analysis the first time she tried Twitter, the time when she'd classified the tweets into buckets of crazy.

"If you think back to that Wilton survey you answered, it did all of the content analysis for you. The researcher decided what the important categories were and translated them into questions. In your case, you're going to let social media decide what the questions are and you're going to work backwards to translate them into the important categories. You can probably already identify some of the main questions, categories like muffins, cupcakes, cookies and squares."

"And cake," Crystal added, having finally figured out what Brooke meant. "Don't forget cake."

"I know you won't let me," Brooke confirmed. "After that, you'll also need to think about subcategories, things like bran, oatmeal, and carrot within the muffin category."

Crystal stared at her buttertart for a moment and then sheared off the entire golden brown edge. "And subcategories for cupcakes would be chocolate, vanilla, and pistachio."

"Sounds perfect. After you've copied all of the pieces of each alert into Excel, read each message carefully and identify the categories and subcategories Make a separate column in your Excel sheet for each subcategory and then tick off the appropriate columns."

"I'll need columns for nut-free and sugar-free too." Crystal reached into her apron pocket for her note pad. From the tweets she'd read so far, she could already think of at least fifteen columns to put in her file.

Brooke glanced at her watch. "It looks like you're anxious to get started so I have one last task for you before I go. I'm so impressed that you used the information you gathered last week to choose a new product to bake. I want you to do it again but, this time, base your decision on the data in your Excel spreadsheet. That's the story I want to hear next week."

Brooke crammed the last of her buttertart in her mouth, gathered up her bookbag from where it had cleaned the floor and slung it over her shoulder. She checked her watch again, and scooted towards the door. "I'm officially late."

"School?" Crystal asked, following her friend to the front of the shop.

"Did I earn my box today?" Brooke asked.

"I beat you to it," Crystal said. "I may have been upset before but a deal is a deal. Your box is right here."

Brooke chuckled and grabbed the box. "You're one sweet cookie."

Crystal waved goodbye and watched the door close, eager to create more Google Alerts. She typed furiously adding a number of different bakeries that she admired and wanted to emulate.

An hour later, a little flashing icon on her screen pulled Crystal's attention away from her task. Bills were always screaming for attention. But she was wrong. Very wrong.

Chapter 9

Crystal was accustomed to getting a few emails every day but three hundred and twelve was ridiculous. Once again, her account had fallen into the hands of spammers. She wondered how many long-lost relatives had died leaving her fifty million dollars that could be claimed by sending them her bank information.

Glancing through the first set of twenty-five emails and then the next twenty-five, Crystal realized the messages did have something in common and it wasn't that they were spam. Every one was a Google Alert.

She opened the first email, a reference to a blog posting about the cupcakes at a bakery on her Twitter list. The next alert was a news article about a celebrity wedding cake. One by one, Crystal browsed through an entire page of Google Alerts. She read about bakeries from across the internet world, from Wordpress and Typepad blog postings, YouTube, MetaCafe, and Vimeo video comments, and Plurk and Tumblr messages.

Crystal knew the internet had millions of websites but this was the first time she had felt its massiveness. The alerts brought her news from websites she'd never heard of before and every one of them had relevant information. The quick read was already turning on more tiny light bulbs of knowledge that she could apply to her bakery.

Just minutes ago, Crystal looked forward to her weekly homework, an easy, speedy task to fill up the hours between waiting for customers, washing dishes, and worrying about her finances. Now she had doubts. She still looked forward to reading the emails but if hundreds appeared in one hour, what would appear in one week.

Determined to put every last ounce of energy into the survival of her shop, Crystal resigned herself to the arduous task. She opened up Excel and created a file with columns for each piece of information in the alerts. One by one, email by email, she copied the author names and dates and links of each message into the appropriate columns.

But by the fiftieth email, the fiftieth date, and the fiftieth link, Crystal regretted setting up so many Google Alerts. She switched her mindset to the second half of her task and set up the second set of columns for the categories she expected to find in the messages. Variables for Squares, Cookies, Tarts, Raisins, Chocolate chips, Mint, Dairy, Gluten, and more were added to the file.

Starting back at the first message and working her way through all fifty messages, Crystal considered the topics of each message and then typed a number one into each of the appropriate columns. Messages about cookies were rewarded with a one in the cookie column and messages about squares received a one in the square column. When the messages included several different topics, Crystal put a one in each of the appropriate columns.

It didn't take long for Crystal to realize that eye-strain would quickly result from the detailed, repetitive work, and she had enough experience with Excel to know there had to be a better way. She could have Excel automatically search for specific numbers and letters and then format them in precise ways.

Crystal grinned to herself as she fiddled with her newly designed Excel shortcut. In a few minutes, she had created a smart function that would search out any occurrence of the word Square and put a one in the Square column. She did the same for the Cookie column, and each of the additional eighteen category columns in her file. In less than ten minutes, every one of the three hundred and twelve messages had been automatically coded according to the baking categories she'd identified.

Genius, she thought. Crystal scrolled down the page to admire her work and make sure every message had been assigned to at least one variable. She added one more column for gluten and finished her task in less than thirty minutes.

"HA," she proclaimed to the quiet bakery. She'd just saved herself hours of painstaking, eye-straining work. Bring on those emails, Mr Google Alerts. Bring them on.

Chapter 10

From inside the bakery, Crystal watched the Crayon Lady approach. Crystal stood still, careful not to make any motion that might call attention to herself. Her heart beat a little bit quicker and a slight grin snuck its way onto her face.

Brooke marched past the bakery window and took a firm hold of the door knob. She stopped, turned her head, and then back-stepped until she stood directly in front of the plate glass window. There, she examined every item displayed in the window. Shielding her face from the sun with her hands and peering inside, she caught Crystal grinning at her, and raised her hand to wave. Brooke returned the smile, and resumed her journey past the front window and inside the bakery.

"Well, well, well," Brooke said, "what have you been up to this week?"

"Do you like it? Do you like it? I love it. I should have done it ages ago. I don't know why I didn't do it." Nervous and excited, Crystal had to admit she was pleased with the result.

"That, my dear, was a smart move." Brooke stood at the cash register and leaned in to get a better look from inside the bakery. "What brought this on?"

"I've read so much about what other bakeries are doing and a giant light bulb came on. Saturday, I picked up the stacks of bills and books and recipes and dumped them all on the table in the back kitchen. When the brownies came out of the oven, I put them in the window right away. And when the cookies and the squares were ready, I put those in the window too. You won't believe it but as soon as I did that, my business doubled. And it's been like that for three days now."

"That's fantastic," Brooke said. "Now that I think about it, it used to be nearly impossible to know from the sidewalk that a bakery occupied this spot. I can't wait to hear the rest of your great news."

"I hate to tell you, but that's the end of the good news." Crystal shook her head. "Putting my baking in the window worked, but the homework you made me do, that failed completely."

"That's disappointing. I've been waiting to hear that story all week." Brooke crossed her arms and gazed across the room. "I had hoped to get a different answer from you. Come, let's settle in." She made her way to the back table, brushed a few crumbs off her chair and sat down.

Crystal followed her with a plate of goodies that she dumped unceremoniously in the middle of the table. "I did exactly what you told me to do. I listened to people from tons of websites and I copied hundreds of the messages into Excel. I figured out what people were talking about and then that's what I baked."

"So where did it go wrong, what happened?" Brooke asked, her brow furrowed in puzzlement.

"What happened is I sent a big box to Daily Bread. Again. It felt good to see business pick up a bit in the last couple of days but that's not going to be enough. Soon I'll be on the receiving end of their business, not the delivering end." Crystal glanced away from the table and stretched her eyes wide, a mostly successful attempt to keep the tears from spilling out.

"I'm sorry to hear it," Brooke said quietly. "Let's see if we can figure out why my plan went wrong. What did your research tell you to make, anyways?"

"These." Crystal vaguely gestured to the plate of chocolate chip squares on the table. "These were the most popular thing in the Excel file. Eat up. No one else is."

"They look good to me." Brooke turned the plate counter-clockwise, examining the chocolate drizzled squares, and finally choosing a square. She took a big bite of the rich, moist square. "And it tastes fabulous. I like the tiny chocolate chips you used. Let's see your work. Let's see if we can figure this out."

Crystal opened her laptop to the Excel sheet and pointed out each section. "Here's my file. These are the messages I copied and these are the columns I made for cookies, squares, cakes, pies, and tarts. You can see I counted up the number of messages for each column. The column for squares had the most messages so I figured I'd make squares. Then, the column for chocolate chips had a lot of mentions too, way more than the columns for raisins and coconut. I put two and two together and made chocolate chip squares. Which no one bought." Crystal picked at her apron string and twirled it around her fingers.

Brooke stuffed the last of the square in her mouth and scrolled rapidly down the page, spot-checking the nicely laid out messages and the perfectly-labelled columns. The summary numbers did indeed indicate that chocolate chips and squares were the winning choices.

Leaning back in her chair, Brooke glanced around the bakery from the bread, to the squares, to the cookies, and back to the category variables displayed on the laptop. "Crystal, try something for me. Go halfway down the file and read the first message in the squares column."

A quick scroll down the file brought Crystal to message number 1652. She read it aloud.

"Had the best date squares today. Stuffed really really thick with dates. Yum!"

Crystal quickly explained. "This one doesn't mention chocolate chips but lots of the other ones do. You saw where I counted that up."

"Understood. Humour me. Read a few more."

Crystal continued reading aloud, pausing briefly between each message, trying to catch any subtle signs that might suggest what Brooke might looking for.

"anyone have a real good pumpkin square recipe I wanna bake something"

"I bought a dozen squares at my kids school bake sale."

"I went shopping in trafalgar square yesterday. It's got a new bakery."

Crystal stopped short. Her finger jumped from the page down button and landed on the screen, smearing a fingerprint directly on top of the word trafalgar square. Brooke, her elbows planted firmly on the table, rested her chin on her hands and smiled.

"Wait a minute," Crystal said, the words oozing from her lips like warm molasses. "Trafalgar square isn't what I meant. That's wrong."

"So how did it get in there," Brooke asked, still smiling knowingly.

"Oh, my gosh, I know exactly how." Crystal sighed. "I knew I wouldn't be able to keep up with all the alerts so I set up a code in my Excel file to search for the word square. I didn't have the time to actually read every single message. I just coded every message. It completely escaped my mind that square meant something other than dessert squares."

"Two things," Brooke said. "First, once again I am impressed with your desire and ability to solve the problem of too much data. When you're dealing with social media data, it's impossible to keep up with the massive volumes of information if you're forced to use a manual system. Automated systems are often the only way to go. Second, everyone who learns about social media research learns this lesson. You spend your days completely immersed in baking date squares and apple squares and pumpkin squares so it's to be expected that it would slip your mind that the word square has other meanings as well. Unfortunately, automated systems, like your fancy little Excel tricks, don't know the other meanings. They won't ask you to clarify if a chocolate square fits into the same category as a trafalgar square."

Crystal turned back to the laptop and, holding her breath, skimmed through more messages coded under Square. Abruptly, she stopped scrolling down the page. She scrunched up her face and sighed, her fear confirmed.

"Here's two in a row." She pointed at the screen again. "These are completely wrong too."

"Eddy finally learned the difference between a square and a triangle. Off to kindergarten we go! But first, a treat at the bakery!"

"The Red Sox squared off against the Seattle Seahawks today. Now I'm going to square off against an apple pie at from my bakery."

Crystal flung herself back into her chair. "Oh, for crying out loud. I tried to save some time with this Excel code and I screwed it up. That's why no one bought my squares. I messed up."

"Hold on, hold on, that's not fair." Brooke leaned in to catch Crystal's eye.

"Maybe not but I'll have to redo that whole column by hand. I didn't have the time to read all of them and now I'll have to do it anyways."

"That is part of the learning process," Brooke said. "Read a few of the messages in the cookie column."

"Oh no." Crystal sat up straight, a look of dread spreading across her face. She knew what was coming. "I messed up that one up too?"

"Read through them and let's see."

Crystal clicked through the messages in the cookie column, desperate to find the error before being forced to ask Brooke to point it out.

"Mmmm, hot chocolate chip cookies right out of the oven. Ouch ouch ouch but still better than going to the bakery!"

"I finished an entire bag of cookies in 2 hours. Now I have to go back to the bakery."

"Cookie monster is my hero! There should be a cookie monster bakery!"

"Cookies drive me nuts. And not the bakery kind."

Crystal stopped reading. She stared at the last message and read it aloud a second time. It made as much sense as carrot cake iced with chocolate ganache and sprinkled with lightly toasted sesame seeds. She turned to Brooke. "How can cookies drive someone nuts? What is this person talking about?"

"You may not realize it, but you already know the cookies they're talking about."

"I'm pretty sure I don't." Crystal pushed the plate of squares closer to Brooke, anxious to see someone eat them if not buy them.

"Let me show you how to find out for yourself. Open up Firefox and find a website called Wikipedia. It's an online encyclopaedia that thousands of people around the world contribute to for fun. You might find a few strange mistakes in there, but for our purposes, it's perfect."

Crystal leaned into the laptop as if seeing the results from ten inches away would magically render the words understandable.

"This is weird. A web cookie?"

"In this case," Brooke said, "a cookie is a little file that saves passwords on your computer so you don't have to remember them all the time, like your Twitter password"

"I almost don't remember my password now," Crystal said. "I don't think I've used it since you made me click that little box."

"Once again," Brooke said, "we can see how easy it is to get so focused on how *you* use words that you forget how other people use those same words. Tell me about the Cookie Monster message."

"At least that one's about cookies," Crystal said, relieved that this one, at least, was correct.

"Are you sure?" Brooke asked. "Why do you say that?" She pulled the plate of squares closer, spinning the plate to bring the one with the most chocolate drizzle directly in front of her.

"Easy. Cookie Monster is a Muppet from Sesame Street and he's always shovelling piles of cookies in his mouth. So there. Cookies." Crystal became less and less sure of herself as she heard the words coming out of her mouth. Something about her answer wasn't sitting well with Brooke. She offered neither a nod of encouragement nor smile of approval.

"Part of your answer is right," Brooke said. "Cookie Monster is a Muppet from Sesame Street and he does eat a lot of cookies. But, tell me, what is the specific idea you were trying to capture in your Excel sheet?"

"I picked out all the messages that had the word cookie in them. This one had the word cookie." She picked up one of the squares and examined the consistency of the crumb. Her hand fell to her lap, spilling crumbs on her otherwise clean apron. "Wait, no. I tried to find messages about cookies that we eat, not computer cookies and not Muppets."

"There we go." Brooke's face lit up as she stretched out her arms in victory. "When people say the phrase Cookie Monster, they are referring not to cookies but to a big blue Muppet who happens to have the word cookie in his name."

"So I have to redo the squares column and the cookie column," Crystal said. "It's looking more and more like all my Excel codes were for nothing."

"Since you're going to redo those two columns, you might want to have a look at the nuts column as well," Brooke said. "Try not to go nuts fixing everything."

Crystal replaced the square on the plate, the edges unmolested. "I keep making stupid mistakes. Is it this hard for everyone?"

"Absolutely. You may have to deal with your own category related problems but everyone doing this kind of research has to worry about the same basic problems. For example, let's say you wanted to paint that huge drab wall behind the dessert case."

"What's wrong with my wall?" Crystal spun around to inspect the wall, its long expanse serving as an ordinary backdrop for her mosaic of perfectly positioned desserts.

"Your wall is fine," Brooke said. "Let's stick with the real issue. In an attempt to choose a better colour for that wall, you conducted some social media research and discovered that there is a lot of chatter about the colour brown."

"Brown? That's horrible. How can brown win over all the other great colours out there?"

"I'd have to agree with you on this one," Brooke said. "What if your research finding sprang out of poor quality data? What if brown generated the most mentions because you failed to think ahead and clean out mentions of Charlie Brown, James Brown, and Dan Brown?"

"Yikes, those aren't colours at all," Crystal said.

"What about black? What if your research concluded black was the most popular colour?"

"I still wouldn't paint it black," Crystal said, shaking her head vehemently.

"But you could sing it instead."

Crystal raised her eyebrow at the odd comment.

"I suspect black is popular," Brooke continued, "but it would be erroneously popular if you failed to remove mentions of the Black Eyed Peas, Jack Black, and Conrad Black. Same for the colour grey. That data could be erroneously full of Earl Grey Tea and grey areas. And the data related to blue might be full of blu-ray disks and blue collar jobs. I could go on forever with examples of how double meanings affect data quality."

"Oh yeah?" Crystal sat up straight and inched her chair forward, a suspicious look enveloping her face. "Is that a dare?"

"Tell you what," Brooke said. "You give me a food word and I'll use it in a way that has nothing to do with food. If I win, I get a double box today. If I lose, I don't get a box at all. Go." She crossed her arms, formalizing the challenge.

Crystal wasted no time. "Savour."

"Savour the moment." Brooke leaned back in her chair with a smug look on her face.

"Bitter."

"Bitter divorce."

"Salt."

"Rub salt into wounds."

"Taste."

"My music tastes have evolved."

"Spice."

"The Spice Girls is my favourite music group." Brooke pretended to hold a microphone to her mouth. "You might as well stop because I'm good at this."

Crystal picked up her chocolate chip square again, resigned to defeat, but more determined than ever to find any hidden mistakes in her work on her own. "I give. I can tell I won't win this one."

"Maybe you can't win this game, but you've certainly won the baking challenge." Brooke brushed the crumbs off her hands. "These squares are wonderful. They've got to be ninety-five percent solid chocolate."

Crystal grinned. Her ability to bake the perfect square was undeniable. Now all she had to do was code a perfect dataset.

Chapter 11

Crystal offered a new treat every week and this time, an almond nougat cookie, shiny with bits of candied fruit and glazed with melted brown sugar, sat provocatively on a plate in front of Brooke. She knew this treat wouldn't last long.

"So far," said Brooke as she reached for the plate and pulled it a few inches closer, "we've spent all our time talking about the contents of the messages but we haven't paid attention to one important thing." She scrolled down the Excel file and pointed to two messages. "Look at these."

"Peanut butter squaress should be illegal. So many kids are allergic to them. My bakery has them right beside everything else and it's dangerous."

"Are you kidding me? Your bakery has carrot cookies? Those aren't cookies. Those are gross."

Crystal chuckled. "Yuck. You'll never find carrot cookies in my bakery. These people don't need to worry about finding terrible things like that at Grannie's."

"So you agree that these two folks aren't particularly pleased."

"I wouldn't say that. I'd say they were definitely *not* pleased."

"Recall when I asked you to identify and make a popular bakery item?" Brooke asked. "Here's my question. Did you include messages like these in your counts? Brooke picked up a cookie and broke it in half. A slice of toasted almond flew onto the table.

Crystal brushed the almond to the floor. Ten seconds. A new record. "I guess I did. I probably shouldn't have counted those."

Shaking her head, Brooke ate a quarter of the cookie. "You do need to include those messages in your analyses but you need to keep track of which ones are negative and which ones are positive. You need to learn sentiment analysis and that, my friend, is our task for today."

"I don't know what sentiment is but you know I'm game," Crystal said. "Bring it on." She rubbed her hands together in anticipation.

"Actually," Brooke said, "you're already familiar with sentiment analysis since you're unconsciously doing it all the time."

"What are you talking about?"

"Sentiment analysis refers to evaluating how positive or negative a word or phrase or thought is. Someone who says they are happy or excited or thrilled is demonstrating a positive sentiment whereas someone who talks about being sad, angry, annoyed, or disappointed is demonstrating a negative sentiment. Any time someone talks or writes, you are unconsciously deciphering their mood, their sentiment. You do the same with everything you read too."

"If that's true, then everyone online is either hugely mad or hugely happy," Crystal said. "Twitter is full of people who are ridiculously angry or excited about everything."

"It does seem like that," Brooke agreed. "But in reality, sentiment on the internet looks a lot like it does in real life. Some of the messages people write are really sad or angry while other messages are really happy or excited. Most of the time, however, they fall somewhere in the middle, somewhat happy or somewhat unhappy, mildly annoyed, slightly impressed, kind of bored." Brooke picked up a second cookie, quickly making half of it disappear.

"I don't know about that," Crystal said. "I've read a lot of stuff online and I don't believe it." She could clearly remember at least two tweets from people annoyingly proclaiming their undying love for KitchenAid mixers. The mixers were good, but certainly not that good.

"That's exactly the point. It's much more fun to pay attention to messages that fall in the extremes. The wild and crazy messages can't help but catch people's attention. Here is your job for the week. I want you to go through your Excel file one more time."

"Because three times is not enough."

"Add a new column called sentiment to your Excel file. Go through every message again and decide if it's positive or negative. How many messages are in your file?"

"Thousands," Crystal said, thinking of the hours and hours she'd spent copying messages into the file and coding the relevant categories. "Oh no."

Chapter 12

It was a relief to have real tasks not make-work tasks but going through thousands of messages yet again was not particularly appealing. After adding a column for sentiment to her Excel sheet, Crystal settled in to read and score as many messages as she could.

"I love the double fudge brownies at the bakery on Elm Street"

"The bread at Wanda's Bakery was nearly burnt. I know they want it dark but I don't like it that dark."

"She gooped icing all over her face, her fingers, and all over the chair at the bakery. It was hilarious! "

This is easier than I figured, thought Crystal, as she skimmed through the first few messages, each sentiment word jumping out like a cupcake eager to be decorated. Her carefully thought out process had her typing a plus one for messages that were positive and a minus one for messages that were negative.

Minus one. Plus one. Plus one. Plus one. Minus one. She scored the sentiment quickly, adding positive and negative words to the dictionary unconsciously building in her mind. Until one message refused to cooperate.

"Stopping at Bread Oven to grab a French bread."

Crystal's finger halted above the keyboard, mid-way between the minus key and the plus key. There was nothing inherently positive or negative, or happy or sad about this message. It was a statement of fact, an observation. She spun her finger in little air circles as she pondered the options. Deleting the message was an option but she had a feeling Brooke would not be pleased with that. Putting it aside until she could ask for help was another option but Crystal was far too independent and far too impatient for that.

But an idea occurred to her. She did have one option left. Crystal wrote a new number in the sentiment column, a number that would reflect no emotion. The absence of emotion. I am that ancient Indian guy, she thought thinking back to her highschool math classes, the guy who invented the number zero.

Armed with a solid plan to handle positives, negatives, and neutrals, Crystal assigned sentiment numbers to more than a hundred messages in her file. But, as the incoming email indicator on her laptop blinked and an hour of the monotonous task passed slower than meringues take to bake, she realized she had a never-ending battle on her hands. She needed a solution that would help her finish the task even if the file grew by hundreds of records every single day.

She stared at the file for several minutes before an idea sparked in her mind. Just as she had used Excel to speed up the variable coding, she would also use Excel to speed up the sentiment coding. But, this time, she had experience on her side. She would be prepared for accidental mistakes that were sure to sneak into her work.

Crystal typed the term sentiment analysis into Google, hopeful that at least one comprehensive list of positive and negative words would appear, a list that would ensure she covered all the possibilities of sentiment words, not just the words she happened to notice. This would be her unbiased data quality assurance. But Crystal was unprepared for the result.

"Holy pie." Her voice was hushed, nearly imperceptible above the hum of the second-hand professional refrigerator tucked around the corner in the kitchen. Thirty-four million results were slightly more than the five or ten she'd crossed her fingers for.

After reading through a few pages of Google results, she was surprised to see she had a choice among several dictionaries of positive and negative words. Unfortunately, a serious problem remained. All of the lists contained thousands of words and phrases, far more than she could possibly manage on her own in an Excel file. Her plan, as great as she originally thought it was, had been dashed.

But the process of reading through the Google results, brought to light a new idea, an opportunity she hadn't realized was available. An interesting phrase had appeared over and over in the results, a phrase which suggested the existence of software that would automatically read messages and assign sentiment numbers – without an Excel file, without human intervention. Indeed, this was better than her original plan and Crystal immediately threw aside her initial disappointment. She had a new plan. A far better plan.

After reviewing the specifications for several of the automated systems, Crystal settled on one that boasted a development team of PhD experts. The system had unmatched quality, tremendous speed, and decades of academic research behind it. And even better, it was free. The baking Gods were finally shining on her.

Crystal followed the instructions on the website and in less than an hour, found herself with a new Excel file containing all of her messages, each one associated with a scientifically generated sentiment score. Even better, the program had coded the messages using the same plus one, minus one, zero system that she had come up with on her own. Yup, she was smart.

Curious about how the software could do the complicated work of a human brain so quickly, Crystal skimmed the first few results. She beamed, pleased that her dive into Google for a simple list had led to serendipitous gold.

"Mmmmm, the cookies at my bakery are delicious!" **1**

"I hate when my bakery doesn't put stuff in the window." **-1**

"There's a bakery across the street from my school" **0**

Seven messages later though, Crystal's beaming face faded into a frown.

Chapter 13

In their makeshift classroom, Crystal shoved the laptop towards Brooke, letting the column of sentiment scores speak for itself. "Look, they're wrong, all wrong." She couldn't help but be disappointed. Tiny little successes along the way wouldn't pay the bills. She needed big successes, and many of them, to turn things around quickly.

Brooke took the laptop, and paged through some of the messages, her eyes quickly scanning from each message to its corresponding score.

Crystal continued her outburst. "Do you see that? Wrong, wrong." She waved her hand vaguely at the laptop. "These are all wrong. There's no way I can score thousands of messages myself, especially since new ones keep coming in every hour, every day. I thought these university geniuses were the perfect solution but they can't do it either. I want to do this but I don't think it's possible." Crystal went limp in her chair, pained at the thought of losing her bakery over such a silly mistake.

Brooke spoke, her voice calm and calculated. "You need to give yourself a lot more credit. You keep impressing me with your determination and ingenuity. To think that there might exist an automated sentiment program that could help you score thousands of messages was a brilliant revelation. We never even discussed that possibility. I do sympathize with you though, over the lack of success you had with it."

"Oh, it wasn't a lack of success," Crystal said. "It was a complete bust. Read the first twenty messages and you'll see right away how bad it is. Five of them are completely wrong so be prepared. I remember how unhappy you were when you found that computer cookie message."

"I'm glad you're taking data quality to heart," Brooke said. "You're quickly evolving into a market researcher who knows that data quality matters. Last week, and without any guidance, I asked you to score the sentiment of your messages and you willingly dove into the task. Now that you have an inherent understanding of how difficult the process is, we can discuss the intricate details of sentiment measurement."

"Great," Crystal said, sarcasm dripping from her voice like strawberry pie in a hot oven. "I only had about eight hundred problems so that should take us about thirteen minutes to get through."

Leaning into the laptop, Brooke typed for several minutes, copying tweets into a new Excel file. Crystal fidgeted and strained in her seat but could not sneak a glimpse. She grabbed the laptop as soon as Brooke made a tiny motion that she had completed her task.

"I am going to ransack your dessert case to fill my treat box," Brooke said as she got up from her seat and wandered behind the counter. "You are going to sit there and score the sentiment by hand for those twenty messages I copied into Excel. Go."

Crystal's heart skipped a beat as she watched Brooke approach the dessert case and slide open the glass door. It felt eerie to see someone rummage through her meticulously organized cases. Finally resigning herself to the fact that Brooke wasn't a tornado, she relented by offering precise instructions. "Use gloves. Under the cash register. And close the glass doors when you're done. And don't mess everything up."

After making sure Brooke's hunting was beyond careful, Crystal turned back to the computer. She prepped her fingers on the one and zero keys and read the messages.

Score	Message
	brownies dipped in sweet mustard? Nommy nommy nommy
	dying right now just looking at these brownies. they're so jacked up.
	Brownies covered in marshmallow & choco chips. That's brekky to me
	Nana and chocolate brownies with vanilla & strawberry ice cream and avocado on top! For two. :)
	What's yer fav snack? — chocolate brownies!
	I make scrummy brownies, thats how it goes.
	Gonna make brownies... Yummy! The sprogs will be toty stoked!

Afer eating my chocolate chip muffin I realized I really wanned brownies
Mmm...warm brownies on a rainy day. Who wants some?
Will do anything for #brownies
#WhoeverIGetWith better gimme a mean massage and bake some good ah brownies
I make 2 batches of brownies.. 1 w black beans... 1 w pumpkin.. neither are cooking properly .. DARNIT!
Her Brownie uniform was still in the dryer so we were late
Waiting for brownies to come out of the oven. Ten oz. of chocolate plus coco powder!
Looking for a yum way to sneak protein into your kids food? You need to make "Black Bean Brownies"
I gotta have molten lava cake, or brownies or chocolate cake... I gotta have something cake like now!!!!!!!
omg I totally just remembered I bought cosmic brownies..
Thorntons brownies are the most addictive things!
Add 1/2 tsp of Watkins Raspberry Extract to a packaged brownie mix for raspberry brownies
yay , Momma LILIANNE Making BROWNIES (; ♥ Yummy

"Hey." Crystal called to Brooke more nervous about the tidiness of her shelves than the validity of her complaint. "I have no clue what some of these words mean."

"Less talking, more scoring." Brooke picked among the remaining squares, topped off her box with a buttertart and tucked the full box into her bookbag at her seat. Quietly taking her seat, she waited for Crystal to finish scoring.

"It isn't fair to put in words I don't know." Crystal was almost finished working through the messages one by one, struggling to read between the lines when words that supposedly meant something were new to her.

"It absolutely is fair," Brooke said. "Perhaps the messages you received from the Alerts didn't contain as much slang as these but I simply copied out the first twenty tweets that used the word brownie."

"Whatever. How'd I do?" Crystal slid the computer with her completed scores across the table.

Brooke instantly blocked it with her hand and whipped her head to the right to stare into the back kitchen. "Stop, stop. Don't let me see your work. Switch it to the second file I created, the blank one."

Puzzled by the frantic request, Crystal did as instructed. "Don't you care which ones I got right?"

"I do but I don't want to see what you've done until I finished scoring these for myself. Then we'll compare our answers." Brooke took the laptop and, far more quickly than Crystal, worked her way through scoring the same twenty items she'd given to Crystal.

As Brooke lifted her hands from the keyboard, Crystal impatiently blurted out her question again. "So how'd I do? How many did I get right?"

"Now we find out." Brooke set the laptop in the middle of the table and copied her own scores into Crystal's file so that their sets of scores were side by side.

Comparing the two columns, Crystal squinched her eyes and shuffled her brows and grimaced at the numbers. "I thought I would have done better than that. I did have to guess at some of them but I'm surprised I got this many wrong."

"What do you mean you got many wrong?" asked Brooke.

Crystal stared at Brooke. "Don't you see what I see? Look at these scores." Crystal pointed to a message to which she and Brooke had assigned different numbers. "You gave this message a plus one but I gave it a minus one. Therefore, I got it wrong."

"*That* is where you're wrong." Brooke tapped the screen. "Unless there are specific words in this message you don't know or don't understand, you cannot assume that my interpretation of this person's message is any more accurate than your interpretation."

Crystal cocked her head in puzzlement. There had to be a right answer and one of their answers, by definition, was wrong.

"Besides, it doesn't matter that we disagreed with each other on these individual scores," Brooke said. "We will always disagree with each other on a small number of scores. Our work here is to better understand where to draw the line when we talk about the validity, the accuracy, of sentiment scores. In other words, it's more important to know that we agreed with each other on sixty percent of these ratings. We can feel fairly confident that at least sixty percent of the sentiment scores we've assigned here are valid."

"Which means forty percent aren't valid. That's a lot of mistakes." Crystal crossed her arms, dejected.

"I won't deny that four out of ten is a lot of mistakes but we only scored twenty messages. What if the twenty messages I selected for our little game were among the most confusing, incomprehensible messages in the entire set of data. It's not fair to judge our accuracy, or the accuracy of any sentiment scoring system, on only twenty messages."

"Let's do another twenty or thirty. I'm up for it." Crystal pretended to roll up her sleeves in preparation.

"I'm thinking more along the lines of scoring one thousand messages, independently, and blind."

Crystal's eyes grew wide. Scoring hundreds of messages was hard enough but scoring a thousand just to find out how good her scoring was? That was a different story.

Without losing a beat, Brooke continued. "If we score one thousand messages without looking at each other's scores, chances are that our scores would generate an eighty-five percent match rate. In the social sciences, that's the number people strive for when they're evaluating human scoring. Eighty-five percent is the standard of perfection, not one hundred percent."

"But fifteen percent of the answers would still be wrong." Crystal wondered how someone so worried about data quality could accept so many mistakes.

"That's how the human sciences work. In traditional market research, people forget which brands they have in their cupboards, which brands they bought at the store this morning, how many jars or cans or boxes they bought last week and that's an error we've learned how to deal with. For this type of research, fifteen percent is the error rate we are willing to accept and we have learned how to work with it."

"I'll have to take you at your word." Crystal wished that angel food cake recipes could be wrong by fifteen percent and still result in a fluffy, spongy cake worth eating in one sitting.

"So let's go back to your original problem," Brooke continued. "You said that the automated program you found on the internet was terrible. Do you still believe that?"

Crystal smiled and wagged her finger at Brooke. "I see what you're getting at. Fine, I give in. I'll have to score a thousand messages by hand and match my scores with the computer's scores. If eighty-five percent of my scores match the computer's scores, then I'll know it's a good program."

"Bingo," Brooke said, "with a slight adjustment. Since you're trying to match human coding with machine coding, you will have to build in some leeway for the additional error associated with automated systems. Instead of eighty-five percent match rate, you're going to want a sixty percent match rate before you can say the program is reasonable or better than chance. If the match rate turns out to be over seventy percent, you can do a little happy dance because you'll have discovered an incredible winner."

"Sixty percent," Crystal exclaimed, her voice raising to middle C. "I thought getting fifteen percent wrong was bad but now you're saying it's fine to get forty percent wrong?"

"Put away that distasteful face," Brooke teased. "There are always trade-offs to be made and this is one of them. Machine scoring may not be as accurate as human scoring but it can score massive volumes of messages in tiny time frames. In the social media space where millions of new opinions are registered every second, you need an automated system that can score millions of messages in mere minutes."

"I had a hard time scoring a few hundred messages in under an hour. You know, after a while, it gets a little boring."

Brooke chuckled. "You've identified another advantage of automated systems. Computers don't find the work repetitive or tiring or boring. The scores they generate are one hundred percent reliable from day to day because they never forget how a specific phrase should be scored, even if it was last scored months ago, and they never accidentally skip over words or miss important phrases. They score every word, every time, and will produce identical scores today, tomorrow, and two years from now. You can't beat the reliability of a machine that doesn't go to the bathroom, go to sleep, or worry about missing American Idol."

"American Idol, that's a song right?" Crystal knew she'd heard it on the radio a few days ago when she was shopping at Loblaws.

"Let's say that. Next week, I want you to tell me if the automated sentiment system you used is great or garbage."

Crystal propped open her eyelids with her fingers. "I'm going to have to buy more toothpicks."

Chapter 14

"I've been waiting to hear your story all week." Brooke perched on the edge of her seat. "I thought about dropping by to see your daily specials in person but somehow I managed to resist. Tell me, what was the result of your validity test?"

Crystal wiggled in her seat, pleased to hear that, for once, Brooke was anxious. "Actually, I'm dying to find out myself. I scored one thousand messages like you said but I didn't calculate the match rate. I waited for you."

"Enough waiting." Brooke leaned forward, her hands clasped together, her eyes jumping with excitement.

Flipping open the Excel file, Crystal typed an equation into one of the cells, and with one finger dangling over the Enter key, smiled at Brooke. "Ready?"

Brooke nodded quickly.

Crystal hit the Enter key.

The two ladies simultaneously bent forward to read the resulting number. And then they both slowly leaned back into their chairs.

Crystal sighed. Her secret wish of doing the happy dance wouldn't happen. The number eighty-five did not magically appear on the screen.

"It's not that bad," Brooke said in a consoling voice. "You passed the first hurdle. We wanted a number larger than sixty and that's what we achieved. You ought to be happy with a match rate of sixty-three percent."

Crystal pursed her lips in dismay. "I hoped for more. You said sixty percent was the bare minimum and this is hardly better."

"Unfortunately, the old adage comes into play. You get what you pay for. But if you think about it, you found a free program that generates a validity score of sixty-three percent. That's fabulous."

"Not fabulous enough."

"If you were paying thousands of dollars for a sentiment system with a validity score of sixty percent, then you would certainly have cause to be annoyed. Quality always costs money, a lot of money. You've done well for a free system."

Crystal responded faster than the disappearance of chocolate chip cookies in a room full of six year olds. "I like free. I can afford free."

"I know that the forty percent error rate bothers you so let's consider some of reasons why that number is so high."

"I still wish it was only fifteen percent, five percent." Crystal produced a plate of oatmeal cookies that was tucked behind the counter and immediately picked one out.

"Hear hear. Unfortunately, it's one hundred percent impossible for any sentiment system to be one hundred percent perfect. Let me give you a couple examples of the worst offenders. Let's say you read a message that said '*I totally love Rebecca Black*' or '*Charlie Sheen is the smartest person I know.*' How would you score those?"

"Easy. Positive." Crystal smiled with smug satisfaction, confident in her new-found sentiment analysis abilities.

"What if I told you that Rebecca Black was a sweet, pretty teenager who made a music video that millions of people ridiculed and criticized? How would you score her message?"

"I didn't know that." Crystal wondered what could possibly be so horrible about the video. "If that's the case, they were probably being sarcastic." She nibbled a raisin off the edge of her cookie. "Wait, maybe not. Maybe that person really did like her. How are we supposed to know the difference?"

"That's the problem. We can't know," Brooke said. "You might have a good chance of scoring it correctly if you were that person's best friend, but the only way to truly know what they meant is to get inside their head. What about the Charlie message? What if I told you Charlie Sheen had a questionable year during which time his behaviour was so strange and unpredictable that people thought he was drunk and doing drugs, a year in which he was fired from the number one comedy show on TV."

"You know I have no time for TV so that's not fair." Crystal shook her finger at Brooke. "But, now that I know, I'd have to say that was a sarcastic message too, a negative message."

"It's tricky, isn't it. First of all, if you don't know the context around a message, it's nearly impossible to know if someone is being serious or sarcastic. And second, if you don't keep up with every bit of pop culture, every bit of news, it's easy to misinterpret the everyday references that affect everything people say and do."

"Which means I'll always miss out on the TV references," Crystal said. "I'll always get the sentiment of those messages wrong."

"And that's alright," Brooke said. "The point is that if you, a human being, find it difficult to interpret something that a human being is trying to say, it won't be any easier for a computer. Sarcasm is a sentiment validity killer whether the data is scored by a human or by a machine."

"I'm the proof," Crystal said, waving her barely touched cookie in the air.

"Here's another challenge," Brooke said. "What was rad decades ago, later became cool, and now is wicked. Language never stops evolving long enough for any one person to completely learn and understand it. Even if you don't recognize certain words, perhaps acronyms, those words could still have sentiment information that needs to be scored. Acronyms are a big part of evolving language and people are getting more creative all the time. One of the most popular acronyms is FTW but if you don't have any context around it, like with sarcasm, you won't know if it means For The Win or Fuck The World."

Crystal grinned at the lackadaisical use of swear words. She could almost feel the soap in her mouth. "I didn't know FTW meant something let alone it meant two different things."

"Two opposite things," Brooke said. "Do you know the meaning of LOL, FTL, WTF, and GTFO?"

"I've seen LOL all over the place. I'm pretty sure it means something funny but I don't know the other ones."

"Well, you're in luck," Brooke said. "This is another place where the internet will help you. One of my favourite websites to decrypt slang and acronyms is the Urban Dictionary. It's similar to a regular dictionary but it's maintained by regular people and it tends to include slang acronyms and words like sick, bomb, and boss."

"What are you talking about? Those are regular words."

"You're awfully sure of yourself," Brooke taunted. "Let me hear you use each of those in a sentence."

Crystal leaned back in her chair, prepared to excel at a ridiculously simple quiz. "I got sick from the flu. A car bomb blew up. I am my own boss. Ta and dum." She emphasized the last words with two firm nods of her head.

"Is that your final answer?" Brooke removed a pair of imaginary glasses and waved them in a circle.

"Absogolutely."

"Too bad. You should know better by now. Just because you have a certain understanding of a word doesn't mean everyone else understands it the same way. Let your fingers do the walking on your keyboard and find the Urban Dictionary website. Tell me how it defines the word Sick."

Crystal manoeuvred to the website and read the strange entry. "This has nothing to do with being sick. How are people supposed to know this?"

"If you were hip and cool, which apparently you are not, you would know. This is a basic example of how language constantly evolves to reflect unique cultures. Pretend, for a moment, that you are cool and use the word Sick in a sentence."

Reviewing the webpage once more, Crystal carefully chose her words.

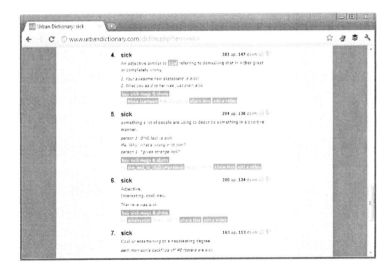

Crystal slammed her hand on the table. "My bakery is *sick*," she said, almost yelling the final word. "That's the best I can figure from this entry."

Brooke burst into laughter at Crystal's dreadful acting skills. "I think you understood the definition perfectly. You and I may know that your bakery is sick but please do *not* tweet that or people will think you mean your bakery will *make* them sick. You don't have the personality or reputation to pull that off."

"Keep reminding me, oh geeky one." Crystal raised and lowered her arms towards Brooke in mock admiration.

"You used to think that sick only had a negative meaning but you'll have to make sure you look at it in context whenever you see it again."

"That seems to be the answer every time we talk," Crystal said. "Anytime I make a mistake, it's because I didn't realize the word could mean something else."

"As does the word bomb."

"Which actually means…" Crystal clicked to another section of the Urban Dictionary website and read the entry. "It means something good. That's so weird. According to this, my bakery is the bomb."

"You didn't pull that one off either," Brooke joked. "There are many words like that, where the alternate use has the opposite sentiment of your original understanding. This, again, is a problem for both manual and automated systems because both methods are completely dependent on someone first identifying the new word or phrase and ensuring it is properly coded. It's another place where data quality errors sneak in."

"Got it, like, OK man, I, like, know what you mean." Crystal realized she may not know all the newest slang, but she could rhyme off old slang with the best of them.

"Precisely. Alright, on to sentiment problem number three. You probably noticed many of these as you scored your messages." Brooke turned back to Twitter and pointed at two messages.

TinaWilburrow
Tina Wilburrow

Love, love, love Cobbs! ☺

Hairy873
Hairy Connie

Brownies suck the big one. ☹

"Yeah, I saw those little smiley faces," Crystal said. "They're cute. I wanna know how to do it." If she had her way, she would put those tiny faces in every tweet.

"The happy and sad faces are obvious," Brooke said. "Like acronyms, these emoticons are simply another way for people to express long or complicated opinions in the short spaces that social media websites often provide. And, similar to acronyms, just because they aren't words and letters doesn't mean we can ignore them. These emoticons have as much sentiment as words like love and hate, and adore and abhor."

"Happy face," Crystal said. "I'd use them too if I knew how to do it."

Brooke typed a few random characters into the Twitter search box and picked through the results. "Have you seen these emoticons before?" She pointed at two more tweets.

WinWen

I hate when my parents ask me why i'm always on the computer. -_-

 BaseballGuy

The bathroom was disgusting *_*

"I haven't seen those before but I can guess what they mean," Crystal said. "And I can see how they did them." Crystal tried to embed the character strings in her brain so she would remember them the next time she wasn't pleased about the winter weather wearing out its welcome.

"Often, all you need to determine the sentiment of a new emoticon is to see it in context. Which brings us to your next challenge."

Brooke pulled the computer close, turned it from prying eyes, and created a small Excel file. She then passed the laptop back to Crystal with a suspicious grin on her face. "Score these. Same rules as before."

Score	Emoticon
	\m/
	(,_,)
	&_&
	(>.<)
	(_/)

Crystal examined the list of characters before her. The confused look on her face said everything. "Um... score what? This is nonsense."

"Au contraire. These are all real emoticons with real sentiment and we both know you are capable of scoring sentiment so go ahead and complete the task." Brooke waved her hand at the computer, pressing Crystal to begin.

Oblivious to the solution, Crystal stared at the screen.

Brooke finally interrupted the silence. "You need some help, don't you?"

Crystal nodded lightly, her fingers poised over the number pad on the keyboard, eager but unable to proceed.

Smiling, Brooke confessed. "Just like all the other website solutions I showed you, there is a solution for this problem as well. Head over to Wikipedia and search for emoticons. Be sure to bookmark that page because you'll use it frequently."

Crystal found the page and scrolled down several times, admiring hundreds and hundreds of unique emoticons.

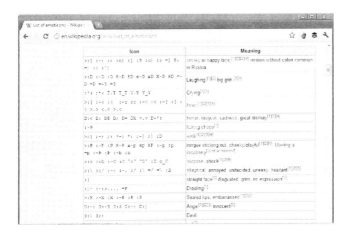

"There are tons," Crystal exclaimed. "And they're so creative. I would never have thought of these but now that I read what they mean, all the little pictures make sense."

"People are ingenious when it comes to making detailed pictures with the characters on a keyboard. And remember, these are only the emoticons that people have thought about adding to Wikipedia."

"I'll never remember all of these but I at least want to know how to do the little smiley face."

"As a human being, you can't remember all of these. But, as you discover new emoticons, you could certainly program them into an automated sentiment system which will always remember the exact sentiment score that belongs to each one. That way, you'll be sure to listen to every single one."

"Do you think there were emoticons in my Excel file that the automated sentiment program didn't recognize?"

"Very likely," Brooke said. "You probably could have improved your sixty-three percent validation score if only you and the computer each had the same understanding of every emoticon."

Crystal tried to remember how many unknown emoticons were in her file. Would fixing them mean she could do the happy dance?

"Are you ready for sentiment scoring problem number four? I'm positive you will find this one is in your dataset," Brooke said.

"Of course it is." Crystal sighed. Every other error Brooke had explained appeared in her dataset so there was no reason for this one to be any different.

"When I walked in today, I noticed you had a new kind of cupcake." Brooke pointed towards the dark chocolate cupcakes taking a prime spot in the dessert case.

"These cookies aren't doing it for you? Sure, I made Devil's Food cupcakes. I sold a few of them over the weekend and decided to try them again today. What do they have to do with my sentiment scores?"

"Pardon me, what was the name of the cupcakes" Brooke had a puzzled look on her face as if she had misheard the name.

"Devil's Food. I know it's not terribly original but my Gramma had such a good recipe." Just thinking about the rich, moist cupcakes made Crystal salivate.

"Do something for me," Brooke said. "Search through your Excel file and find a message about Devil's Food.

Crystal typed a few words into her computer and produced a message. "It says:

'Devils food cake is lishous when they double the chocolate chips and drizzle it with extra chocolate.'

"That does sounds delicious," Brooke said. "I could eat one right now."

"Help yourself." Crystal knew that Brooke's random comment wasn't really a comment but a subtle question about treats. For everything Brooke had done so far, she was more than happy to play along. "My cupcakes are the bomb."

"Smart cookie. How would you score this Devil's Food message, positive or negative?" Brooke wandered behind the counter, placed two cupcakes on a plate, and returned to their workspace.

"Positive for sure." Crystal watched Brooke choose the two cupcakes with the tallest icing. "That message makes me wonder whether I should forget the icing and drizzle them with hot chocolate syrup and chocolate chips instead."

"Drizzle or not, these look licious." Brooke licked off the icing that had fortuitously smeared over her fingers. "Find the sentiment column and tell me how that message was scored."

"Just… a… sec…" Crystal ran her finger along the screen, lining up the message with its score. "Wait, this must be wrong. Why is this scored negative?" She peered up at Brooke, waiting for the answer she knew would come.

"Ah, yes."' Brooke pointed at a single word in the message. "This is your problem."

"Oh, for crying out loud." Crystal slapped her hand against her forehead. "I didn't notice that. Devil. That's just the name of the cupcake. It doesn't actually mean a devil." She watched as Brooke pushed half of the cupcake into her mouth, completely erasing any essence of professionalism that may have previously existed.

"We keep coming back to the multiple meanings of words. It affects how we collect our data, how we code our data, and now it's affecting how we score our data."

"Same mistake, different pile." Crystal wondered how many more ways double meanings could mess up her work.

"Have you ever realized how many brand names have sentiment words in them? For example, most people would love to be a King or Queen with all the money and power in the world but Burger King and Dairy Queen are simply restaurant names. The same goes for Ace hardware, Bounty paper towels, and Free and Clear detergent. Those are simply brand names that happen to have words we normally associate with positive sentiment."

"Maybe they pick those words to make us secretly think the product is better than it really."

"There's no denying the effort that goes into choosing a brand name with subliminal messaging but many brand names are simply descriptions of the brand or organization. The American Cancer Society is a wonderful charity that raises money to support cancer research, cancer detection, cancer treatment and cancer education. It doesn't matter how horrible cancer is, messages about the ACS shouldn't be scored negatively just because the word cancer is in their name."

"I'm starting to wonder how my file managed to be sixty percent accurate," Crystal said. "There are so many problems with sentiment that maybe it's an impossible game."

"Sometimes I wonder too," Brooke agreed. "If language stayed constant throughout the decades and centuries, humans and machines would have an easy time with sentiment analysis. Unfortunately, it evolves so quickly that it regularly confuses both people and computerized systems. One misstep and your research results and conclusions will lead you down the wrong path."

"Like my cookies and squares."

Brooke nodded her head. "Exactly." She checked her watch. "Shoot, I'm late. I have to get going." Brooke shoved the second half of the cupcake in her mouth, gathered up her things and pushed her chair in.

Typical student, Crystal thought. She always hated when her classmates dribbled in one by one, minutes after class had started, disrupting everyone and wasting time. Brooke seemed to make a habit of it. But then Crystal remembered something.

"Wait, wait. You haven't told me the one thing I actually want to know. You can't go yet."

Brooke paused to swallow the last of her cupcake. "You have a one track mind." Brooke scooted to the front door. "It's easy. Type a colon and then a parenthesis. Your PC will flip it into a little smiley on its own."

Crystal grinned. Of course.

Chapter 15

"Sixty-seven." Crystal waited impatiently for Brooke's reaction. Brooke hadn't asked her to do it, but she'd had the entire week to do the work and find out.

"Sixty-seven what?"

"I'm so disappointed. I thought you would know what I meant right away. I re-checked my scores from the sentiment system based on everything you told me last week. I looked for wrong emoticons and words that I misinterpreted. Sixty-seven is my new validity score." The work had taken many hours, with many visits to the Urban Dictionary and Wikipedia websites, but those four additional points meant that when Crystal rounded off the number, it became a seventy. She much preferred the sound of that.

"Impressive. I can tell you're happier with that result. Are you ready for something new in the sentiment department?"

Crystal nodded, pleased with herself.

Brooke copied five messages from Twitter into a new Excel sheet and passed it to Crystal. "Here's a brand new set of messages for you to listen to and score."

Score	Message
	The brownie was good, not the best, but good.
	It was a little burnt. I didn't like it all that much.
	I stopped by Magnolia's today.
	OMG that's a barbie cake! I wannit for my birthday pleeeeeeeasse
	I want cake, ice cream, chicken, peach cobbler, pepperoni pizza, kool-aid, pasta, BBQ, cookies, muffins, Chinese food!!

"No problem. I'm good with this now." In a minute, Crystal had scored one neutral, two positive, and two negative messages. She turned the laptop back to Brooke, pleased with her newfound understanding of slang and emoticons, and proud of her increasing speed and accuracy.

Brooke barely glanced at the scores before rendering her conclusion. "I would have done that differently."

Crystal spun her head back to her scores. "What? Which ones? These are all right." Clearly, Brooke needed to look at her work with a bit more care.

"It's not that I disagree with your scores in general but as I listen to the intent of those messages, I would have done it differently. You're ready to take your scoring expertise one step further."

Brooke took the laptop, added a column to the little table, and typed in five scores of her own.

Crystal examined Brooke's numbers. "Type the emoticon for surprise because that's what I am. I didn't think about the messages being anything more than positive, neutral, and negative. But I can see there's more to it."

"You figured out my secret code," Brooke said, folding her fingers together in the sneaky manner of Spy vs. Spy. "Just like the system you found, many of the automated systems out there score sentiment the way we have. Negative, neutral, positive and nothing more. But that doesn't accurately reflect the world we live in where there aren't just three ways to feel. Decimal places let us assign numbers like 0.5 to messages that are somewhat positive, 0.8 to messages that are very positive, and 1.0 to messages that are astonishingly positive."

"Same for negative message too, right." Crystal tried unsuccessfully to wipe a pinky finger-sized smudge of icing off of her apron.

"You've got it. There is an infinitesimal number of decimal places between minus one and plus one which means there is an option for every emotion that exists."

"How do you know if something is a 0.5 or a 0.8? Aren't those basically the same?"

"Therein lies the problem," Brooke said. "Listening is highly subjective. My idea of what is slightly positive is guaranteed to be different from yours. You might assign a 0.3 to a message that I think better deserves a 0.4. Unless you use an automated system which always scores messages consistently, there will never be a perfectly reliable answer, just a well-thought out, logical answer, hopefully grounded in concrete rules."

"Rules like what?"

"One of the basic techniques is to pretend you're answering a survey question that uses a five point Likert scale." Brooke flipped through the messages on the computer screen and pointed to one. "Listen to this message here."

> *I kinda likes the cinnamon oatmeal cookies at the bakery on the corner.*

Brooke pointed to the beginning of the message. "Let's rephrase this message as a survey question."

> *What is your opinion about the cinnamon oatmeal cookies at the bakery on the corner?*

"Assuming we're using a five point scale," said Brooke, "the possible answers would be very negative, somewhat negative, neutral, somewhat positive, and very positive. If you listen to the intent of the message, how would you answer that survey question so that it matched the original message, so that it matches *Kinda Like*?"

"*Kinda Like* is positive."

"Listen to it carefully. How positive?"

"I'd say not very positive but it is somewhat positive. That would make it a 0.5." Crystal wondered how many times

Brooke had used the word listen so far today. The Crayon Lady nickname was seeming less and less appropriate.

"I like that choice," Brooke said. "The decimal places come into play when you feel that a round number doesn't quite reflect the intended sentiment, when you think that *Kinda Like* might be slightly more than or slightly less than Somewhat Positive. Is it a 0.4 or a 0.6? That's where the subjectivity comes into play."

"I'd leave it at 0.5. I think it's right in the middle. Hey, why do we need all this precision anyways?"

"Let me give you three scenarios," Brooke said, "and then you tell me which one you want for Grannie's Goodies.

> Scenario #1: Fifty people feel positively about your shop
> Scenario #2: Ten people love your shop and forty people like your shop
> Scenario #3: Forty people love your shop and ten people like your shop"

"Number three, number three," Crystal said with the excitement of a four year old child placing her order at McDonald's. "I want the one where forty people love my shop."

"And that is why we like scoring with decimal places," Brooke said. "It's important to know whether people like or dislike your shop, but it's far more important to know whether people like or love your bakery. The people who like your shop might occasionally stop by if they're in the neighbourhood but the people who love your shop will visit you again and again, and they'll go out of their way to shop at your store. They will even recommend your shop to their friends." Her eyes followed Crystal as a plate of cupcakes materialized from behind the counter and landed on the table.

"Pistachio," Crystal said. She loved watching Brooke's eyes widen when a plate of treats appeared on the table. She always wondered how quickly each option would capture her attention and make her lose her train of thought.

Brooke tore her eyes away from the plate. "Let's score another message with a continuous sentiment scale. Try this one."

 BillWhelan

I stopped at Cobs today

"Also easy," Crystal said. "Neutral. He didn't say he likes or hates Cobs. He didn't say it rocks or blows. He didn't put a smiley face on it. It's just a boring comment."

"That's one way to look at it," Brooke said, "but you and I are looking at sentiment from a specific point of view, from the view of a shopkeeper. Did this gentleman have to go to Cobs? I doubt it. No one *needs* to go to a bakery. He could have made his own bread or bought some at a grocery store, pharmacy, or corner store. If he didn't care what bakery he went to, he could have just said he stopped at a bakery. So why did he specifically say that he went to Cobs?"

"He happens to know the name," Crystal said. "No big deal." She wondered how long it would take Brooke to break down. Would it be minutes or seconds before a pistachio cupcake met its maker?

"Perhaps, but the question still applies. Perhaps the reason he said the name is because he has a slight positive emotion towards Cobs. If that's it, then how would you score the message?"

"Well, I would have given it a zero before but I'm thinking it should be more positive than that."

"Perhaps a 0.5?" Brooke picked up a cupcake and peeled the paper cup off the cupcake creating a little pile of crumbs on the table.

Crystal smiled, her gaze following the crumbs from table to floor where Brooke brushed them. "I don't think so. If I use that licking scale you mentioned-"

Brooke burst into laughter. "Likert scale, it's a Likert scale. As in Like and then Ert."

"Okay, Madam Dictionary. If I use that Likert scale you mentioned, it's more than zero but it's less than 0.5. Maybe a 0.1?"

"That works," Brooke said. "Whether you assign it a 0 or a 0.1, it's important to first consider your research objective. Are you measuring generic sentiment, or are you measuring sentiment with a specific goal in mind, within the context of consumers and shopping. Let me give you another example along the same lines. How would you score the phrase *I bought bread at Cobs.*"

"Maybe 0.1? It doesn't have sentiment either but it does mention a brand name."

"Remember that sentiment belongs in context and you're a shop owner," Brooke said. "How does it feel to know that someone purchased an item in your store?"

"Awesome," Crystal said. "Have another cupcake. As awesome as two big, fat, cupcakes."

"So you'd assign a one to that message?" Brooke folded up an empty cupcake cup and dropped it back on the plate. Her eyes remained on the plate.

Crystal scanned Brooke's face for a clue to the right answer, though she saw nothing but a longing for more sugar. "Yes?"

"I think no," Brooke said. "Now you're thinking about the context too much. The message is positive, but certainly not to the degree of a one. If you give that message a one, then you have nowhere to go when you find a message that says *I like buying bread at Cobs*. Even worse, you've got nowhere to go when you find a message that says *I f-ing love buying bread at Cobs*."

"Which means *I buy bread at Cobs* is more than 0.1 but less than 1," Crystal said. "Maybe 0.5, along the lines of somewhat positive or somewhat agree." Crystal felt her brain expanding every week, that soon it would burst with all the new things she had learned.

"Bingo," Brooke said. "You're a great student. Ready for one more lesson?"

"Yuppers." Bring it on, Crystal thought. Even if the bakery failed and she lost every penny, at least she'd have everything she'd learned from Brooke to help her get back on her feet.

"Alright, pull out your Excel file and let me see the thousands of messages you've coded and scored. Sort the messages into alphabetical order and page down until you get to messages that start with the letter R. What do you see?"

"Oh, shoot," Crystal exclaimed as she examined the results. "I accidentally copied the same message in here a bunch of times. Gimme a sec while I delete them." She highlighted the messages and raised her finger over the delete button.

Nearly tipping over her chair, Brooke jerked forward and pushed Crystal's hands away from the keyboard. "Wait, wait, wait. Those are not mistakes. I knew there would be many duplicate messages there."

Crystal withdrew her hands to a safe distance. "You don't have to jump all over me. There is an undo button, you know." She looked at the message and back to Brooke. "How did you know those duplicates would be there? And so many of them?"

Brooke relaxed back into her chair. "Sorry, a bit of data geekness escaped there. Who wrote those messages?"

Crystal scrolled over to the appropriate column and examined the usernames. "It's all different people. And on different dates. How are all these people saying the exact same thing?" She ran her finger down the screen looking for more examples of the strange occurrence.

"It's the magic of Twitter." Brooke wiggled her fingers in the air like a close-up illusionist. "Actually, most social networks have a feature like this. They call it retweeting or sharing or buzzing or liking or plus one but in all cases, it's a way to help people share messages that they think are meaningful or funny or useful or interesting. One click of a button and the network will automatically copy and post the message on your own profile."

"I've done that a couple times." Crystal remembered a picture of the most beautiful braided Rye bread ever she'd ever seen, glossy dark brown and perfectly symmetrical. She couldn't help but click on the retweet button so that all of her followers could enjoy the photo too.

"It's common particularly when people are talking about celebrities. Watch, I can find one in two seconds." Brooke typed a few words into the Twitter search box and turned the screen to Crystal.

 **Belieb4ever**
I love justin bieber

Retweet thsi if you love Justin Bieber

"Typo alert." Crystal planted a fingerprint on the screen which she quickly wiped off with the edge of her apron. She had to stop doing that. The screen looked like one giant smudge with a light sprinkling of flour and icing sugar.

"There are thousands of these." Brooke scrolled down the page as tweet after identical tweet filled the page, differentiated only by the name and user photo. "This person is a fan of Justin Bieber, one person among millions of other obsessed fans. It's fun for them to create a tweet and see how many people will share their message. That one single tweet could easily generate five or ten or twenty thousand identical tweets, each one of them appearing on the surface to be a duplicate message."

"Who is Justin?" Crystal had a faint feeling that she ought to know. Twenty thousand tweets had to mean something.

"If you're older than twelve, you don't need to concern yourself with him," Brooke said. "Back to your datafile. You could delete all of those duplicate messages but then you would be left with one opinion from one person. Instead of knowing that thousands of people love Justin, it would look like only one person loves him."

"Which is wrong," Crystal said.

"And we're in agreement again. It's important to know if ten thousand people are in love with Justin or if one person is in love with Justin. And similarly, we need to know whether two people or two thousand people are retweeting your recipe ideas and pictures of your baking."

"People really like retweeting pictures. I've got to tweet more drooly pictures."

"You are full of those."

"Of what?" asked Crystal.

"Crystal words. You build on the Crystal language dictionary every week. I would never be able to score your tweets properly."

Chapter 16

Books, pens, and papers lay spilled on the floor where Brooke had dumped her bag. She stood in awe, her gaze darting from one spot to another on what had once been an immense wall of monotonous sheetrock. No longer plain, no longer dull, and no longer blandly invisible, the bakery combined artistic beauty with the smell of warm oatmeal bread mixed with a dash of fresh latex paint.

Anxiously standing beside her, Crystal waited as though on a bed of coals, her toes twitching, and excitement bursting from every pore on her body. "What do you think? What do you think? Do you like it?"

Brooke finally managed to breathe in and force the air through her vocal cords. "That is absolutely stunning." She looked at Crystal and back at the wall again. "You did this? By yourself?"

"Yup." Crystal felt like a first time mom presenting her new baby to friends and family, full of pride and joy and exhilaration. "I used to do odd painting jobs for people. I painted a giraffe on my cousin's bedroom wall and the numbers on the door of her house. And you've seen the Grannie's sign I painted over the door. I just never painted anything this big."

What had once been an unforgiving expanse of dreary wall had been transformed into a field of graceful wheat under a sky of peaceful blue. A vast haze of wheat ready for harvest graced the lower half of the wall. Warm skies of marshmallow soft clouds ushered peace and tranquility to the bakery. Crystal was no longer the owner of a bakery that displayed bread and treats, but the master of a warm and comforting space to nibble on warm brownies oozing with creamy dark chocolate icing.

"This is absolutely stunning," Brooke said, her gaze unbroken. "I cannot believe you did this. Where did the inspiration come from?"

"I knew you'd love it," Crystal exclaimed. "You started it when you called my bakery boring. And then, I read my data and I kept seeing messages about how some bakeries look so sterile. All the white walls and shiny counters look clean but people want clean and yummy, not clean and hospitally. I counted how many of those messages were positive and negative, and that's all I needed. I always assumed that people wanted my bakery plain and uncluttered but my data said there is such a thing as too clean."

"Research comes to the rescue again," Brooke said. "We like to think we have all the answers, but it's completely unreasonable to think one person can know everything. One person is a biased research group."

With one more long look at the wall, Brooke smiled at her friend. "I'm glad to see you're still an artist because artwork is on the agenda for today. Are you ready?"

"You brought paint?" Crystal tried to peer into Brooke's bookbag, beyond the books scattered on the floor, but no paintbrushes or paint tubes were to be seen. Just more books. Brooke really needed to add a few more classes to her schedule if she had enough free time to read all those books.

"Look all you want, there are no paintbrushes in there."

Crystal grinned, slightly embarrassed to be caught sneaking a peak into the bookbag. She grabbed her laptop, a plate of goodies, and the two ladies settled themselves at the table.

"The art we're going to do is online with a website called Wordle." Brooke opened the laptop and clicked her way to the website. "There are lots of other sites, like Tagxedo, Tagul, or Wordsift, but Wordle made this art form accessible and it's still the one most people are familiar with. Ready?"

Crystal took over the laptop and clicked on the Create Your Own button.

"Let's start simple," Brooke said. "Copy one hundred messages from your Excel file, paste them into Wordle, and let's see what happens."

An artistic arrangement of words resulted, small, medium, and large in variations on the theme of auburn.

"Oh cool!" Crystal grinned and leaned into the word cloud, squinting and tilting her head to read the tiniest words. She turned to Brooke. "It's really pretty. What does it mean?"

"It's simpler than you think. Word cloud programs like this split sentences into their individual words and then display each word depending on its frequency."

"That explains why the word bakery is so huge and IKEA is so small," Crystal said. "I'd be suspicious if IKEA was the big word. What does the colour mean?"

Brooke sighed. "That's a popular question with an unpopular answer. First of all, the colours make it easier for your brain to separate the words. When two words are side by side, it's easy to accidentally read them as a single phrase rather than two distinct words. And second, a black and white word cloud would lead to the same conclusions, but it wouldn't be nearly as attractive. For the most part, the colour is there to be pretty and, sometimes, pretty is what counts."

"I like pretty," Crystal said. "And it's about time we did something that wasn't page after page of numbers."

"Well, this bit of fun is going to help you learn more about the demographics and psychographics of your consumers so you can market to them better. We've already determined that you aren't able to use a survey to learn about the demographics of your non-existent consumers, but we can try to discover that information another way."

"From pretty pictures." Crystal highly doubted that pictures, as lovely as they were, were the best way to learn about people who liked bakeries. But, she conceded, she did have less experience with this than Brooke.

"From pretty pictures," Brooke confirmed, her voice as confident as always. "Tell me what you see in that word cloud."

"I'd have to say most of the messages use the word bakery. But they have to or they wouldn't be in my Excel file."

"That is actually a good validity check," Brooke said. "Make sure that the word cloud makes sense and then you can move to the next step. Now, go beyond the obvious."

"It's like a Where's Waldo of baking. I guess people talk a lot about sugar, flavour, dessert, cupcakes, flour, and sweet. You know what? There aren't many conversations about the bread side of things. It's mostly the sugar side of things."

"Good catch," Brooke said. "You've just extracted your first insight from a word cloud. Your Excel file can tell you exactly how many times each of those words were used but word clouds are a quick way to visualize the results in one glance, a quick way to get a feel for the overall contents of a set of data."

Crystal turned back to the Excel file to grab another set of data. She couldn't wait to see what else hid in the data. "Lemme do another. This is cool."

"Let's take a different tactic this time," Brooke said. "Our goal is to learn who our consumers are and this word cloud is a bit too generic to be useful. This time, sort your Excel sheet so that all the messages using the word cupcake are at the top. Make a word cloud out of those messages."

After a few clicks of the keyboard, Crystal hit the Enter key with a flourish. "Done and done."

"This is so cool," Crystal exclaimed. Her eyes dashed back and forth, up and down from word to word on the screen. "You know what I see in this? Red Velvet cupcakes. I've never made them. Maybe I should. And look here, raspberry comes up a lot, and pink, and sprinkles." Turning to Brooke, Crystal pursed her lips and crinkled her eyebrows. "You know what? This word cloud is a list of things I need to add to my Excel file. And bake."

"Well, given what we learned about the negative mentions of cookies, I wouldn't bake them yet," Brooke said. "These word clouds don't tell us whether people love or hate

Red Velvet cupcakes but rather that people talk about them. You will need to add them to your Excel file and measure the sentiment properly before you decide whether baking them is the right decision."

"I managed to forget that," Crystal said, slightly embarrassed. "I got distracted by the pretty pictures." She preferred to forget the failed chocolate chip squares and the failed tea biscuits, and think positively. Pull it all together, she thought.

"Fluff happens," Brooke said. "Ready for another way to use word clouds?"

"Yuppers."

"This time, we won't concern ourselves with what specific cupcake or cookie or square people are interested in."

"Then what's left?" Crystal asked.

"What's left is paying attention to how people speak. The college kids who wander past your shop all the time may be speaking English, but it's not formal, professional English. We're going to become linguists for a few minutes and explore who is taking about bakeries based solely on the words they use." Brooke took the laptop from Crystal, selected a new set of messages, and generated another word cloud.

Tilting her head to make sense of it, Crystal noticed the word cloud did little to explain the world of baking. Even worse, it did nothing to help her figure out who the speakers were. "I have no idea what messages you chose for that word cloud but it's just a bunch of random words."

"It's definitely not a bunch of random words," Brooke said. "See the words gonna, yeah, ahh, nomnomnom, Mmmm, and smileeeee? What do you think of those words?"

"They're positive words? Is that it?" Crystal said.

"That's a correct observation, my budding linguist, but not the one I wanted. This word cloud tells you that your consumers are comfortable using slang. And that's not a universal finding."

"They use slang. How does that help me?"

"A couple of ways. First, if you're interested in creating marketing materials, maybe a flyer, a website, or even signs in your shop, you'll want to make sure that the language you use corresponds with the language your target audience uses. This word cloud tells you that it's acceptable to use casual language. You don't have to use slang, but neither do you have to use highly professional and exactingly perfect grammar."

"Like you do." Crystal grinned thinking about Brooke's overly professional language. She had enough data to figure that Brooke wasn't a regular college student. She had to be a mature grad student.

"Second, sometimes, the type of slang people use represents a unique group of people, a sub-culture. Try this. Look at the slang words in the word cloud again and draw a picture in your head of the people it reminds you of. What kind of person are you imagining?"

Crystal leaned back in her chair, stared at the water pipes edging the ceiling, and wiggled her fingers on the table. The word cloud wafted through her mind and she pictured the words flowing out of the mouths of people. Their faces, bodies, and clothes morphed in and out as she tried out various options. "I'd have to say they're young people, maybe the same age as me."

"You came up with the same picture as I did," Brooke said, nodding. "Let me show you another word cloud along the same lines."

"That's practically the same as the last one. It's a lot of slang, a lot of young people talking."

"It is slang but it's a particular type of slang. Look closer at some of the strange words."

Crystal examined the word cloud for a second time. "Tryna? What's that?"

"That's not the only strange word in there. I see lov, smh, gr8, lmao, shud, ur." Brooke pointed out each word as she spoke.

"I can find out what those mean in the Urban Dictionary, right?" Crystal said.

"Now we're talking. That's the best place to start. Not only do we see generic slang within the vocabulary of people who like to talk about bakeries, we also see that our bakery fans are comfortable using chatspeak or textspeak."

"That's part of demographics, liked age or gender, right?" Crystal asked. "How do we find out whether boys or girls are talking about bakeries? How do we do that?"

"That's where we turn to language in context," Brooke said. "Let's put the word clouds aside and look at some whole messages." She turned back to Twitter and hunted around for a few messages. "If you look at these tweets, you can't tell from the name or the pictures whether they are men or women, but you still know who is talking."

 **WickedPickins**

My wife always forgets to buy english muffins

 ChrisWatson

Fuccin piecea burnt cookie

 Swirlup

Ruined my new dress last night. Spilled strawberry pie all down the front. ☹

Crystal read through the tweets. "This is a man talking about his wife and this is a woman is talking about her dress. But the other one, I can't tell."

"Why not?" Brooke asked. "It actually has the person's name."

"You can try to trick me but I'm on to you now. Chris could be Christopher or Christine. There's no way for me to know if it's a guy or a girl."

"Actually, luck would be on your side if you guessed a man," Brooke said. "Both women and men use a lot of profanity, but statistically, in the online space, men are more likely to swear."

"Really? Something new all the time." Crystal thought back to all the messages she'd read so far, trying to remember if men did in fact swear more than women. She'd be sure to check that out for herself.

"That logic applies to other demographic characteristics as well. People who have higher incomes might be more likely to talk about owning or buying luxury products by Lamborghini, Gucci, Versace, or Armani. People who have lower incomes might be more likely to talk about buying second-hand vehicles, renting less expensive apartments, or being anxious to get their paycheque. It's definitely not a perfect method but when you've exhausted all other options to learn about your target market, you've got to rely on the available techniques."

"I could even set up my Excel sheet to do that," Crystal said. "I could pick out messages that have swear words, or mention boyfriends, purses, or earrings."

"Whenever you have time, it would be worth it," Brooke said. "That covers off the demographic information but it still leaves us the psychographics, a potentially more important topic than demographics. One last thing you can do with your dataset is look for topics that have nothing to do with baking. Identify which TV shows your consumers mention, which celebrities, sports, or cars, they mention. All of these seemingly irrelevant topics will give you a better idea about who your consumers are, what interests them, excites them, and annoys them. The more you know, the easier it is to market to them."

"Sports? Cars? How will knowing people like sports cars help me sell more bread?" Crystal asked. It made a lot of sense now, she thought. The same word kept coming up. Brooke had to be a marketing student.

"Those little details will help you fine-tune the things you bake, how you decorate your shop, when you have sales and promotions. For instance, if you learn that people talking about bakeries are interested in baseball -"

"- then I could sell baseballs in my store." A tiny smile crept onto Crystal's face as she imagined a pile of baseball cupcakes, iced in blue or red depending on the home team colours.

"That's a possibility, but you could make cookies and ice them to look like baseballs. What if you found out that people who like bakeries are also fans of the television show Ace of Cakes?"

"Easy," Crystal said. "I could bring in a TV and have those shows on in the background. Actually, maybe I should do that." She turned around, looking for the perfect spot. She had a TV slowly disappearing behind a pile of recipe books at home that she could bring in.

"That works," Brooke said. "You see, once you know more specific things about your customers, you can find new ways to appeal to them. You can plan your baking schedules around them and know exactly what kinds of things will attract them to your shop."

"There is only one group of people I want to attract right now," Crystal said.

"What group is that?"

"People with money in their pockets."

Chapter 17

Brooke dragged a chair over to the table, brushed the crumbs off the seat, and sat down. A plate stared back at her. "You must have a huge Excel file by now. How many rows are in it?"

Crystal opened the file. It didn't have every Google Alert she'd ever received, but it did have enough messages coded and scored to create a three megabyte file.

"37 314," Crystal replied, a proud look on her face. In other words, hours and hours of mistakes and fixes and puzzles.

"Lovely," Brooke said. "Because we're going to need every last piece of information in there and every last thing you know about Excel."

"Awesome." Crystal shuffled her chair closer to the table, eager to dig into today's lesson.

"You've been collecting messages for how long now, two months?"

Crystal held up two fingers and nodded. "Yup. I can't believe it's been that long."

"We've come a long way, baby," Brooke said. "I need you to make more columns in your file."

"Seriously? How many this time? My file is going to explode." Crystal pictured little numbers and codes spewing high into the air, tiny ones and twos and threes covering the table and chairs and floor, and mixing in with the brownie crumbs on the floor.

"I think we can risk it," Brooke said. "Give me three more columns in that file. Name two of them after your favourite bakeries and one after my favourite bakery."

"Which one is your favourite?" Crystal asked as she prepared the columns, surprised Brooke actually knew any bakeries. She had never seemed interested in other bakeries before.

"Your bakery, young lady," Brooke said. "Wake up, wake up."

Laughing, Crystal set up the requested columns and added two more for bonus points.

"Tell me this," Brooke said. "Which bakery generates the most online conversations? And don't guess, I want facts based on data."

"I *can* guess because I know the answer is Magnolia's," Brooke said smugly. "I've read enough messages over the last few weeks to know."

"So prove it." Brooke swept her arm over the laptop. "Prove it."

Crystal examined the first row in her spreadsheet, the row set up to count the number of messages in each column. But it didn't give her the answer she expected. Magnolia's wasn't the top bakery. Where Magnolia's had 389 mentions, two other bakeries had 609 and 478 mentions. Two competitors had snuck by without her noticing.

"It's not Magnolia's," Crystal said with suspicion in her voice. Worried she'd made yet another mistake, she double-checked her code. "Nope, that's right. Magnolia's is only the third most popular bakery. Franella's is the most popular bakery." She was disappointed to have missed such a simple thing. She straightened her apron, not even bothering to brush off the specs of icing stuck to it, and tucked a few stray hairs back behind her ear.

"You read the messages every day yet it didn't register with you that Franella's was the most popular one," Brooke said. "You see, it doesn't matter how unbiased you want to be, the human brain is incapable of pure logic. That's one of the advantages of your Excel sheet. It can't be swayed or distracted by any of your preconceived notions, your likes or dislikes, your preferences, hopes, or dreams."

"I guess I did get caught up with Magnolia's. I want Grannie's to be as popular as they are. I'd like to see line-ups outside my door every morning." Crystal's eyes fell as she pictured Magnolia's in her mind, the large, spacious bakery always staffed with at least five cheerful part-time staff.

Brooke picked up a cookie and bit off the section unfairly stuffed with chocolate chips. She let the chocolate melt on her tongue before continuing. "Do you have a lot of experience building charts in Excel, enough to create complicated bar charts and line charts?"

"Yuppers." Crystal smiled, happy to see the chocolate chip cookies had done the trick. "Excel charts are great for procrastinating. I've made a ton of charts to figure out my huge costs and tiny sales and I'm ready for something different."

"Perfect. Then this will be easy. Start with a simple chart that shows the total number of mentions generated by each of the bakeries you identified."

"No problemo." With a few quick keystrokes and a suspicious grin, Crystal presented her work. "Done."

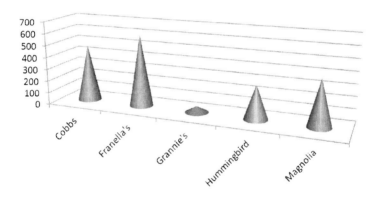

Brooke threw her head back in loud laughter and raised her hands defensively. "Stop, stop. That hurts."

"What's wrong," Crystal asked, a look of great pain and embarrassment on her face. "You asked for a chart. I made a beautiful one for you."

After a deep breath, Brooke responded in her normal calm voice. "I'm sorry about that. I didn't mean to jump all over you. Let's keep things clean and simple. No 3D. No fancy colours. Alright?"

Crystal's barely perceptible grin turned into a cheeky smile and she turned back to the keyboard. She had guessed correctly. Brooke did not approve of fancy, schmancy when it came to charts. Changing the style of the chart to a vastly more boring option allowed Brooke a moment to recover.

Number of Bakery Mentions

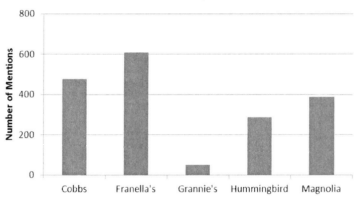

"Much better." Brooke returned the smile. "This is a chart I can read without getting a migraine. You've passed the first test which means you're ready for something more difficult."

Shimmying her chair closer to the table, Crystal prepared to accept the oncoming challenge, however unreasonable it may be.

"A couple of months ago, we talked about sampling, the process of deciding from which websites you would collect your data."

"I remember that," Crystal said. "That's how my dataset got so big. It's got messages from a ton of websites I'd never heard of before."

"Now we can bring that discussion to life. Tell me, what percentage of your dataset comes from Twitter?"

Crystal clicked through her file and calculated the answer. "Almost half. Forty-five percent." Crystal stopped for a moment and thought back to the long-ago discussion. Something didn't make sense. "I thought you said only fifteen percent of internet users are on Twitter?"

"Someone paid attention," Brooke said. "You've identified the problem for yourself. Your dataset is overwhelmed with opinions from people who prefer to chat in short, quick messages."

"But we still have thousands of opinions from everywhere else, so it's not all bad, right?"

"As long as you understand how severe the problem might be. Chart something for me."

Crystal raised her hands over the keyboard, ready to create the next masterpiece.

"This time, I want to you to compare not bakeries, but websites. I want you to chart the average sentiment of messages sourced from five of the most popular websites and explain to me what you see."

After a collaborative effort, a new chart emerged. Crystal rested her chin in her hands as she examined it. She remembered being told there were differences among the websites but at the time she had assumed Brooke was exaggerating to make a point. Now she saw differently.

Average Sentiment By Website Source

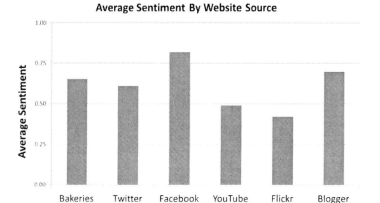

"People on Facebook are a lot happier about bakeries than people on Flickr."

"Right," Brooke said. "On average, across all of the messages and all of the websites, the average sentiment about bakeries is about 0.65. Since the range goes from very negative at minus one to very positive at plus one, bakeries are generally getting a good score. But, opinions from Twitter, YouTube, and Flickr are more negative and they pull the overall score down while opinions from Facebook and Blogger are more positive and they pull the overall score up."

"Why are those Flickr people less happy? Don't they see all the gorgeous pictures I see?" Crystal had an epiphany. She imagined a Grannie's Flickr account, overflowing with colourful pictures of her own sweet successes. She had hundreds, maybe thousands, of baking pictures that could only generate positive opinions about her store.

"That's an important question. If your research objective requires that you focus your attention on one specific website, Flickr for instance, you would need to explore your

Flickr data in more detail to answer that question. What exactly in the Flickr data is associated with lower sentiment? And with that knowledge, how could you counter-act it in how you run your bakery?"

Crystal nodded. She wondered if Flickr accounts were as easy to maintain as Twitter accounts.

"But, if you're focused on overall sentiment across a wide spectrum of the internet," Brooke continued, "you would need to make sure that you aren't led astray simply because your dataset is focused on one particular website. Don't let Twitter opinions distract you from your focus because they are vastly different from other opinions."

"I'll probably spend most of my time chatting on Twitter," Crystal said. "Maybe it's OK that I have an extra helping of Twitter data."

"If it matches your research objective, then that's a good decision. I've got another complicated chart in mind so pass the laptop back." Brooke set up a new table of sentiment scores, but instead of breaking out the scores by the name of the bakery or the website source, she broke out the scores by weeks.

Crystal eagerly anticipated the subsequent task. "Let me at that," she exclaimed, taking charge of the laptop and creating a line chart.

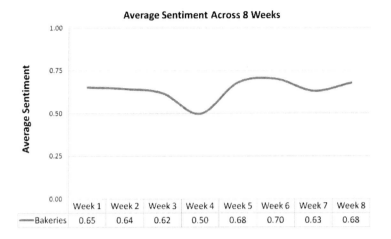

	Week 1	Week 2	Week 3	Week 4	Week 5	Week 6	Week 7	Week 8
Bakeries	0.65	0.64	0.62	0.50	0.68	0.70	0.63	0.68

"Now you're the psychic one," Brooke said. "Explain this chart to me as if don't know anything about Excel or sentiment or research."

Talking mostly to herself, Crystal hummed and hawed, and chose her words carefully. "This chart shows sentiment about bakeries since we started our meetings." She turned the laptop three millimetres to the left as if that would make the chart easier to understand. "It shows that sentiment was always positive, always good, and how it went up and down a little from week to week. Over eight weeks, average opinion towards bakeries was kind of even. They didn't change much except for that little drop in week four." Crystal peered out of the corner of her eye at Brooke.

"You're a pro at this. It's unfortunate that we can only track the last two months," Brooke said. "Google Alerts doesn't provide historical data but if you had some budget, you could purchase older data from a third party supplier and recreate these charts going backwards in time, before you realized that you wanted to do this research. Now that would be psychic."

"Cobs is thirty years old," Crystal said. "I could have had a chart with thirty years of data."

"Let's see." Brooke smiled and tapped her fingers together. "The internet was a baby thirty years ago and you weren't even born, email became usable in the 90's, and Facebook, YouTube, Flickr, and Twitter were only born in the last few years. Given that, I'm going to say that charting the last thirty years of online sentiment towards Cobs isn't possible."

Crystal groaned, embarrassed that she hadn't figured it out for herself. "But the last five years would work. Since Twitter and Facebook?"

"Even that's iffy," Brooke said. "If you think about who used social networks five or even three years ago, and how they used social networks, those people reflect a unique group of keeners and early adopters and computer geeks. Recently though, social media and social networks have been adopted more generally and it's a place where average people spend their time. With that in mind, it would be fair to chart the last year of sentiment towards Cobs, but no longer than that."

"I can't imagine what I would do with more than a year anyways," Crystal said. "I like to live in the present. I can work with a couple months of free messages. What do we do now?"

"This chart tells us how people talk about bakeries in general. You saw what I did, yes?"

Crystal nodded her head.

"Make me proud and add two more lines to this chart. Show me the average sentiment over time for these two bakeries."

A few minutes of numerical nimbleness passed before Crystal dropped her hands to her lap. "Done."

Average Sentiment Across 8 Weeks

	Week 1	Week 2	Week 3	Week 4	Week 5	Week 6	Week 7	Week 8
Bakeries	0.65	0.64	0.62	0.50	0.68	0.70	0.63	0.68
Magnolia	0.72	0.69	0.74	0.79	0.6	0.85	0.76	0.76
Franella's	0.47	0.41	0.44	0.36	0.45	0.56	0.5	0.57

"Very impressive," Brooke said. "Your Excel skills are almost on par with your baking skills. Once again, tell me what this chart means."

Crystal grinned, and then knotted her hands together in thought. She examined each point in detail before revealing her official conclusion with proud confidence.

"People consistently like Franella's more than the average bakery -"

"Wait right there, Sherlock," Brooke said. "Are you reading that correctly?"

Puzzled, Crystal dragged her finger across the top line on the screen and read the legend again. "Oh my gosh, I can't believe I did that. I assumed that since Franella's had the most mentions it also had the most positive scores."

"That negativity might have been why you failed to realize it generated the most messages," Brooke said. "People often conclude that many mentions means many good mentions but over the last year, numerous companies have been the victims of massive volumes of conversations that were actually massively volumes of negative conversations."

"Like who?" Crystal wasn't interested in the negativity but she was eager to know how the companies had generated massive volumes of conversations.

"Well, you might recall a massive oil spill in the Gulf of Mexico. It generated millions of extremely negative tweets and blogs."

"The Brad Pitt, basis points, blood pressure problem," Crystal said, thinking back to their earlier discussions.

"Your memory is impeccable. Toyota and Ford also had to deal with millions of negative conversations when they decided to recall their vehicles. Product recalls for popular consumer products almost always result in massive volumes of negative conversations. The moral of the story is never make assumptions about your results based solely on the volume of messages."

"Like I did," Crystal said. "Again. But this is the last time. I promise." She scrunched her hands into five pairs of awkwardly crossed fingers as proof.

"You didn't finish explaining this to me yet." Brooke gestured to the chart.

"I was so rudely interrupted," Crystal said, a smile on her face. She turned back to the chart and carefully noted from the legend that Magnolia's was the top line, Franella's was the bottom line, and general mentions of bakeries were reflected in the middle line. "Magnolia's has more positive sentiment than the average bakery. People like it more than average."

Brooke smiled and nodded.

"And Franella's has less positive sentiment than the average bakery. Too bad for them. But it looks like something happened to Magnolia's in week five. I don't know what but it wasn't good."

"You might want to extract Magnolia's data for that week and attempt to determine what happened. Perhaps she introduced a new product that people didn't like or ran a promotion that wasn't well received. You'll want to make sure that something similar doesn't happen to you. Build another chart for me."

"No problemo," Crystal said. "You know I can do it."

"Add one more bakery to that chart. Yours."

Instantly excited, Crystal dug into the data. After two minutes though, she withdraw her fingers from the keyboard. "This isn't going to work," she concluded sullenly. "Those other bakeries have tons of data and I have barely fifty. I should have put my tweets in this file so I'd have something to chart."

"First of all," Brooke said, "You've just told me that you have fifty messages in your datafile that mention Grannie's. Has it sunk in that people are starting to talk about your bakery? This is fabulous news."

Crystal smiled, shyly proud of her accomplishment.

"And second, it was a smart decision not to include your own tweets. You already know what your own opinions are. You need to understand the opinions of other people."

"That still leaves me without a chart. There's only a few messages for Grannie's and it wouldn't be fair to chart them." It would make a lot more sense to read them in the Excel file, Crystal thought. Who makes a chart when the number of messages can be counted using your own fingers and toes?

"I love that attitude," Brooke said.

Crystal was puzzled. On what planet was a pessimistic attitude a good thing?

"You made the right decision not to create a chart for your shop. Charts made with insufficient data are one of the leading causes of deceptive trend lines, incorrect conclusions, and automobile accidents."

Crystal jerked her head to the side, positive she'd misheard.

Brooke smiled. "You're such a good student. We're going to make an exception to the sample size rule today and create that chart anyways. We're going to learn from it."

"Whatever you say." Crystal prepared the pitiable chart and presented it to Brooke with little enthusiasm.

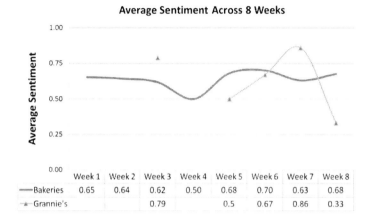

Average Sentiment Across 8 Weeks

	Week 1	Week 2	Week 3	Week 4	Week 5	Week 6	Week 7	Week 8
Bakeries	0.65	0.64	0.62	0.50	0.68	0.70	0.63	0.68
Grannie's			0.79		0.5	0.67	0.86	0.33

"This is perfect," Brooke said. "We're lucky. Even though charts based on fewer than fifty messages in each time slot are not to be trusted, this chart will serve us well."

"Even though half of it is missing?" Crystal remained unconvinced and unimpressed with the half-empty chart.

"Let's look at week one. During this week, we see regular chatter about bakeries. And, during that week, you barely knew what social media or Twitter was, tweeting wasn't your strong suit, and no one mentioned Grannies in the social media space. This week tells the truth, the whole truth, and nothing but the truth. Look at week 3."

"The dot." Crystal rolled her eyes, completely unimpressed.

"Right, the dot. At least one person mentioned your shop that week. And it was positive. The sentiment was higher than the average score for bakeries."

"Oh gosh, I forgot about that. Woo hoo." Crystal raised her hands in the air in self-congratulation. MovieDaniel had never replied to her private message so she had left the framed tweet in the back kitchen where she could enjoy it while she baked every morning. But it didn't matter. She still loved that tweet and smiled at it every day.

"You should be excited," Brooke said. "That was the week you started to feel confident with Twitter, the week you started to feel comfortable chatting online with people, asking questions, answering questions, and participating in the social media community."

"It's kind of neat how those weeks match up. Cool." Crystal began to see the light.

"There's another point in here that matches up." Brooke pointed to the highest point in the chart, week seven. "This is the week you painted your gorgeous mural and you received all those compliments from your Twitter friends."

"This chart is a map of everything I've done. It's keeping track of how good I'm doing. Neat!" Crystal was so excited she could barely sit still.

"Neat, that takes me back. Don't let this go to your head though. This chart is still based on far too few data. It's not reliable at all."

"But maybe in a few more weeks it will be?"

"For sure. Last chart before I go. Do the same thing as before, track sentiment through the weeks, but this time I'd like to see a comparison of cupcakes and buttertarts."

With several charts of practice under her belt, Crystal produced the chart quickly. Without waiting for Brooke's request, she immediately described the results, curious to learn the result, eager to know if her baking strategy would match the outcome.

Average Sentiment for 8 Weeks

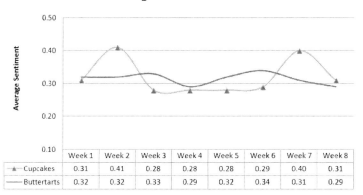

	Week 1	Week 2	Week 3	Week 4	Week 5	Week 6	Week 7	Week 8
Cupcakes	0.31	0.41	0.28	0.28	0.28	0.29	0.40	0.31
Buttertarts	0.32	0.32	0.33	0.29	0.32	0.34	0.31	0.29

"The average sentiment for buttertarts is above zero, which means it's positive. People like them. Same for cupcakes. But the sentiment for buttertarts is really flat while the sentiment for cupcakes goes up and down. That's strange." Crystal paused, staring at the two lines doing two different things. She tried to imagine why they would be so different but came to no conclusion.

"What kind of cupcakes do you make every day?" Brooke asked.

"I don't make the same ones every day at all. Sometimes chocolate, sometimes vanilla, sometimes pistachio. You really liked the pistachio ones. Sometimes I go crazy and make a random recipe I find on the internet."

Brooke sat quietly.

Crystal waited, hoping for the smallest hint. A second passed before she realized she didn't need a hint. "I get it. People make different cupcakes all the time. They might make one kind one week and a different kind another week. Some of them are winners and some of them not so much. But buttertarts, well, one buttertart is pretty much like another. Changing the nuts or the drizzle still leaves you with the same buttertart so people are generally happy all the time."

"I'm starting to wonder if you need me anymore," Brooke said. "That's a great hypothesis and you'll need to go back to the raw data, the qualitative data, to see if your hypothesis is correct. Either way, you'll learn what causes people to be more or less happy about cupcakes."

Crystal grinned, pleased to hear she was doing well. "And once I learn that, I can make sure I apply it to my store. Make sure I don't make the same mistakes."

"Keep up with your work," Brooke said. "As you continue to tweet, you will attract more people to your store, and you'll be able to measure the progress of your bakery and all things Grannie. You'll be able to select out messages mentioning individual kinds of cupcakes and cookies, your different kinds of bread, your artwork, and anything else people want to chat about. You'll be able to track the ups and downs over time for every item in your shop. The charts, and what you learn from them, will only be limited by your imagination."

"Don't worry." Crystal tingled inside, thinking about all the possibilities. "I think I caught the Twitter bug." She couldn't wait to know what hundreds of people thought of Grannies even if they didn't tell her in person. She wanted to know which cupcakes people liked the most and the least, whether they liked the egg wash or the milk wash on the whole wheat bread. She loved having a window into the minds of not one person, but many people. She envisioned a better bakery, one built not on guesswork and assumptions, but on knowledge and understanding. A bakery based on research.

Chapter 18

Brooke stepped out of the community library with a fresh batch of Canadian biographies. She'd nearly finished reading that entire section of the library and would have to move to another one in the next couple of weeks. She stood in the middle of the sidewalk, a drop of sunshine dancing lightly on her forehead, and admired the random patches of sunlight that pushed through the patchwork of clouds. Now in full leaf, the maple trees shaded the steady flow of pedestrians enjoying the warm spring weather.

She slung her bookbag over her shoulder, and meandered down the street lost in thought. Some days, she felt like a two-faced imposter. On the outside, she worked hard to appear confident, all-knowing, and cheerful. That's what a mentor needed to be to instil confidence and excitement in others.

On the inside, though, self-doubt filled her heart. She worried that the fear was obvious to others, that they could tell the hope and optimism were more desire than reality. College was the best place to learn theory, but when someone's livelihood was on the line, theory was not sufficient.

The last couple of months of helping Crystal had felt good, really good. She genuinely needed and deserved the help. But life held no guarantees. As Crystal said herself, chatting about social media and playing on the computer was no substitute for good old fashioned, nose to the grindstone hard work.

Even worse, Grannie's wasn't a major store with a large footprint on the main street of a major city. It was a tiny bakery in the middle of a neighbourhood that people hurried through on their way to somewhere else. Any failure would be Brooke's failure for interfering in something that was not hers to touch, for not recommending to Crystal that she get out while she still had something to take with her.

Brooke continued down the sidewalk until she could proceed no further. A herd of college kids who needed to take a class in sharing the sidewalk chose this moment to disregard her desire to pass through. The herd blocked the entire sidewalk and entrance to the neighbouring shop, completely ignoring anyone who had a ridiculous idea of passing by or going inside.

"Move aside, you trouble makers," Brooke said with exasperation. Mumbling, the herd gradually parted leaving a path barely wide enough for Brooke to squeeze through. She found the door to the shop and pushed inside. The narrow entrance was packed with college kids talking over each other and holding debit cards in hand. Pushing her way in, Brooke took her place at what she could only assume was the end of the line.

Now this, she thought, was a happy place, a place anyone would want to visit, a store to be proud of. Brooke noticed a familiar face through the crowd and raised her hand in a slight wave.

The motion caught Crystal's attention. With a huge grin on her face, she waved in return. She nudged the person beside her, whispered a few words, and made her way to Brooke.

"I've been waiting for you," Crystal said. "You haven't been by in a few weeks and I was wondering what you've been up to, if you've missed me. How's everything?" She took Brooke's hand and pulled her into the back kitchen where the chatter of the customers faded slightly.

"I've been good," Brooke said. "More importantly, it looks like you've been good too."

Crystal's face told the entire story. She beamed. "I'm not good. I'm great. Look at this." She waved her arm towards the crowd. "Forget one hundred customers. Think hundreds of customers. We blew that research objective out of the water. After you taught me about psychographics, I made flyers to leave at the college. And, I set up a Flickr page showing new pictures of my baking every single day. Those pictures get tons of retweets and lots of people ask me for cupcake advice. I even changed the shape of my oatmeal bread and watched the sentiment for it improve almost immediately."

Crystal waved her arm at the chit-chattering crowd. "This is because of you. I could have never done this without you."

"You could have never done this without social media research," Brooke said. "I've noticed that you've been charging ahead in social media without my assistance. I saw your facebox page."

Crystal giggled. "And I found you on the tweeter. I know who you are."

"I even clicked on the like button." Brooke pretended to click a little button in mid-air.

"I saw that," Crystal said. Pointing at the dessert case, she reminded Brooke. "I owe you several forgotten treat boxes from the last couple of visits. Let me go fix you a box right now."

"Definitely not," Brooke said. "This is a busy shop and I'm a paying customer." She glanced at the crowd which was only getting larger with one less person serving them. "You have a lot of customers to take care of and your new employee isn't keeping up with demand. It's good to see you but the chit chat must wait."

Crystal grinned and scooted back behind the counter where she immediately helped the next customer in line.

On the receiving side of the counter, Brooke bumped her way back to the end of the line. She couldn't see past the elbows and hands and phones into the dessert case. It was a mystery what new things Crystal had baked as a result of her new-found research skills.

"Excuse me, pardon me." Brooke tapped the shoulder of a young man in front of her, furiously talking with a friend. "Is this the end of the line?"

"Yeah," he said, turning to see who had interrupted his conversation. A smile of recognition erupted on his face. "I didn't expect to see you here. By the way, class yesterday was awesome. I've never stopped by for office hours but I wanted to tell you that I actually look forward to class every week to see what happens next in your case study."

"I'm glad you're enjoying it," Brooke said, finally placing the young man's face. He always traipsed into class at least ten minutes after it had started, disturbing everyone and making her lose her train of thought. Tardiness was not to be tolerated.

The young man continued talking eagerly. "You know, you should try that case study out with a real store. See if your social media research technique works in real life. That would be sick."

"Maybe I will. Maybe I will." Brooke smiled. Being a college professor had its rewards.

The End

The Listen Lady's Two Favourite Recipes

F. Annie Pettit

Lazy Bread

3 cups flour
1.6 cups water
1 tsp (1 package) yeast (any kind)

Variations
Add a tbsp of your favourite flavouring such as garlic, dill, basil along with the flour

Mix the ingredients together in a medium sized bowl. Cover the bowl with a tea towel. Let sit, untouched, for at least 12 hours, preferably 18 hours. Turn into a greased loaf pan or onto a greased cookie sheet. Bake in a 400 degree oven for 40 minutes. Remove from oven. Wait 5 minutes. Eat the whole thing.

F. Annie Pettit

OMG I Need Cake Now
or
5 Minute Cake in a Mug

3 tbsp flour	1 egg
3 tbsp cocoa	1 tbsp sugar
3 tbsp milk	1 tbsp oil

Variations
Add a tbsp of chocolate chips, nuts, or other treat along with the other ingredients

Mix ingredients well in a coffee cup. Put the cup in the microwave and cook on high for 3 to 6 minutes depending on the power of your microwave. It will rise in the cup and possibly look like it's going to overflow. Don't worry. It won't. Remove from the microwave. Get a fork. Eat the whole thing.

ABOUT THE AUTHOR

ANNIE PETTIT, PhD is Vice President, Research Standards at Research Now, and Chief Research Officer of Conversition. With the Conversition team, she was one of the first in the market research industry to develop a scientific, quantitative methodology for social media research. Annie is an author of the ESOMAR, CASRO, MRA, and MRIA social media research guideline. She tweets at @LoveStats and writes the LoveStats marketing research blog where her sweet tooth occasionally shows itself.

http://lovestats.wordpress.com
http://ca.linkedin.com/in/anniepettit
http://twitter.com/lovestats

Chat with other Listen Lady readers on Facebook
http://facebook.com/TheListenLady

F. Annie Pettit

The Listen Lady